The Wright Brothers

Bessie Coleman

Charles Lindbergh

Amelia Earhart

Benjamin O. Davis, Jr.

Neil Armstrong

Sally Ride

DARING
American Heroes of Flight

9 Brave Fliers

Eileen Collins

Most Daring Deed:

Trailblazing NASA Astronaut Who Became
the First Woman Space Shuttle Pilot and the
First Woman to Command a Shuttle Mission

MyReportLinks.com Books
an imprint of
Enslow Publishers, Inc.
Box 398, 40 Industrial Road
Berkeley Heights, NJ 07922

Jennifer Reed

MyReportLinks.com Books, an imprint of Enslow Publishers, Inc. MyReportLinks®
is a registered trademark of Enslow Publishers, Inc.

Library of Congress Cataloging-in-Publication Data

Reed, Jennifer, 1967–
    Daring American heroes of flight : nine brave fliers / Jennifer Reed.
        p. cm. — (Great scientists and famous inventors)
    Includes bibliographical references and index.
    ISBN-13: 978-1-59845-081-1 (hardcover)
    ISBN-10: 1-59845-081-6 (hardcover)
    1. Air pilots—United States—Biography—Juvenile literature. 2. Aeronautics—History—Juvenile
literature. I. Title.
    TL539.R44 2008
    629.13092'273—dc22
                                        2007031817

Printed in the United States of America

10 9 8 7 6 5 4 3 2 1

To Our Readers:
Through the purchase of this book, you and your library gain access to the Report Links that specifically back
up this book.
The Publisher will provide access to the Report Links that back up this book and will keep these Report Links
up to date on **www.myreportlinks.com** for five years from the book's first publication date.
We have done our best to make sure all Internet addresses in this book were active and appropriate when we
went to press. However, the author and the Publisher have no control over, and assume no liability for,
the material available on those Internet sites or on other Web sites they may link to.
The usage of the MyReportLinks.com Books Web site is subject to the terms and conditions stated on the
Usage Policy Statement on **www.myreportlinks.com**.
A password may be required to access the Report Links that back up this book. The password is found on the
bottom of page 4 of this book.
Any comments or suggestions can be sent by e-mail to comments@myreportlinks.com or to the address on
the back cover.

♻ Enslow Publishers, Inc., is committed to printing our books on recycled paper. The paper in every book
contains 10% to 30% post-consumer waste (PCW). The cover board on the outside of each book contains
100% PCW. Our goal is to do our part to help young people and the environment too!

Photo Credits: Associated Press, pp. 60, 74; American Academy of Achievement, p. 95; CAIB Photo by Rick
Stiles 2003, p. 90; CBS Broadcasting Inc., p. 86; City of Elmira, p. 106; The Franklin Institute, p. 15; Library
of Congress, pp. 10, 12, 16, 32, 34–35, 40, 42, 46, 50, 52, 57, 72; NASA, pp. 19, 78, 82, 89, 92, 108, 111,
114; NASA Headquarters – GReatest Images of NASA (NASA-HQ-GRIN), p. 97; NASA Kennedy Space Center
(NASA-KSC), pp. 87, 104, 110, 113; NASA Marshall Space Flight Center (MASA-MSFC), pp. 76, 99;
© Dr. Russell Naughton 1998-2007, p. 24; The Ninety-Nines, Inc., pp. 48, 58; Office of the Secretary of
Air Force (Public Affairs), p. 71; Purdue University Libraries—Archives and Special Collections, p. 54;
Shutterstock, pp. 26–27, 68–69; Smithsonian Institution, p. 102; Smithsonian National Air and Space
Museum, pp. 5, 6, 14, 63; © Underwood & Underwood/CORBIS, p. 20; U.S. Air Force photo/Senior Airman
Christopher Boitz, pp. 8–9; U.S. Centennial of Flight Commission, p. 30, 44, 65; WGBH Educational
Foundation, pp. 17, 22, 37.

Cover Photo: NASA Headquarters – GReatest Images of NASA (NASA-HQ-GRIN)

CONTENTS

MyReportLinks.com Books
Great Books, Great Links, Great for Research!

The Internet sites featured in this book can save you hours of research time. These Internet sites—we call them **"Report Links"**—are constantly changing, but we keep them up to date on our Web site.

When you see this "Approved Web Site" logo, you will know that we are directing you to a great Internet site that will help you with your research.

Give it a try! Type http://www.myreportlinks.com into your browser, click on the series title and enter the password, then click on the book title, and scroll down to the Report Links listed for this book.

The Report Links will bring you to great source documents, photographs, and illustrations. MyReportLinks.com Books save you time, feature Report Links that are kept up to date, and make report writing easier than ever! A complete listing of the Report Links can be found on pages 116–117 at the back of the book.

Please see "To Our Readers" on the copyright page for important information about this book, the MyReportLinks.com Web site, and the Report Links that back up this book.

Please enter **DHA1528** if asked for a password.

Introduction

*I*t has only been a little more than a hundred years since humankind invented the airplane. In a short time, humans did not just make it to the skies. We also invented planes that go faster than the speed of sound and rockets that launch people into outer space.

No book on aviators would be complete without the story of the Wright brothers. After all, they invented the plane. Many aviation dreamers came before them, but no one was able to get a machine with wings off the ground and in the air. In 1903 the Wright brothers did just that.

This Smithsonian National Air and Space Museum Web site profiles women who have broken the gender barrier to become famous pilots and astronauts.

EDITOR'S CHOICE

Access this Web site from http://www.myreportlinks.com

Suddenly, for all the people who dreamed of flying with the birds, their dream had come true.

Men and women have overcome great odds to fly. However, in the early days of aviation, mighty flying machines were flown by men only. Flying was very dangerous and not considered safe for women. Yet, some of the greatest pioneers of the sky and space to date have been women, including Bessie Coleman, Amelia Earhart, and Sally Ride.

When Amelia Earhart was young, women were expected to become housewives or teachers, never

The **Black Wings: African-American Pioneer Aviators** site tells the story of African-American aviators who paved the way for racial equality "in the cockpit" through profiles and an archive of images.

aviators. But Earhart had a mind of her own, and she was determined to not just fly, but also to break records. Among her many achievements was being the first woman to cross the Atlantic with two other men, as well as being the first woman to cross the Atlantic alone. Her final 29,000-mile trip around the world would have been a triumphant moment, had she made it.

Amelia Earhart's courage to fly enabled other women to take to the skies and beyond. Sally Ride thought becoming an astronaut would be an incredible experience. She studied and worked hard, stuck to her astronaut training, and became the first woman in space.

The fight for fairness, equality, and the right to become a pilot was especially difficult for African Americans. So when Bessie Coleman wanted to fly, most people did not think it would happen. Yet, she became the first African-American woman to fly. She performed daring stunts in her airplane and wowed crowds. Coleman also wanted to open a flight school so that other African-American women could have the chance to fly.

Benjamin Davis, Jr., faced the same discrimination. While in the Army, he was purposely belittled and given the silent treatment because he was African American. He knew he could prove that the country needed him as well as many other African-American aviators. They proved themselves worthy

Women began serving as Air Force combat fighter pilots in the mid-1990s. Here, Captain Kristin Hubbard checks the landing gear of her F-16 Fighting Falcon fighter jet.

and often better flyers than many of the all-white squadrons. Davis was part of a group of men called the Tuskegee Airmen. They were the first black military airmen.

Although there are many great aviators, this book highlights nine very special people. All had a dream to fly and all were determined to reach that dream through perseverance and hard work. At great risk—even at the cost of life—these brave men and women made the desire to fly a reality for the world.

The Wright Brothers

Ever since Wilbur and Orville Wright were young boys, they loved machines. In 1878, when the boys were eleven and seven years old respectively, their father brought home a small windup toy operated with a rubber band. It was called the Penaud helicopter, named after its French inventor, Alphonse Penaud. Penaud came up with the idea of using rubber bands for power. This was the Wright brothers' first introduction to a flying machine.

The boys loved their new flying toy so much that they made copies of it. They called it the "bat." It always flew well, but when they made a larger version of the

Orville Wright

Wilbur Wright

Lifeline

1867: Wilbur Wright born in Millville, Indiana, on April 16.

1871: Orville Wright born in Dayton, Ohio, on August 19.

1892: Open the Wright Cycle Company.

1896: Begin to make their own bicycles.

toy, it did not. They did not understand at the time that the larger the flying craft became, the more power it would need to fly.

▲ BOYS WITH BIG AMBITIONS

Wilbur was born on April 16, 1867, in Millville, Indiana. He was the third son born to Milton and Susan Wright. Milton Wright was a minister. He moved the family to Dayton, Ohio, where Orville was born on August 19, 1871. A daughter, Katharine, was born three years later. The Wright family lived at 7 Hawthorn Street in Dayton, Ohio.

Orville's career as an inventor began at an early age. When he turned twelve, he and a friend published a school newspaper called *The Midget*. Eventually Orville built his own printing press. When he was older, Orville started a weekly paper and hired Wilbur to be the editor.

1902: Glider travels more than 622 feet on October 23.

1906: U.S. Patent office grants a patent for their flying machine.

1948: Orville Wright dies of a heart attack on January 30.

1900: Begin experimenting with gliders at Kitty Hawk, North Carolina.

1903: The Wright Flyer makes the first controlled, powered flight on December 17.

1912: Wilbur Wright dies of typhoid fever on May 30.

Wilbur was quieter in nature than Orville. He liked athletics and loved to read. One of the games he liked to play was called shinny, which is like hockey. In 1886, when Wilbur was almost nineteen years old, a player on the other team let go of his stick. It hit Wilbur in the face, knocking out several teeth. During his recuperation, Wilbur spent a lot of time reading books about the flight experiments of Otto Lilienthal and Octave Chanute, two pioneers of human aviation.

BOOMING BICYCLE BUSINESS

In the late 1800s, the bicycle industry was booming. Wilbur and Orville decided to set up their

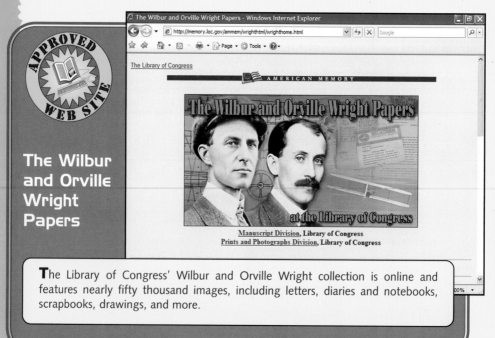

The Wilbur and Orville Wright Papers

The Library of Congress' Wilbur and Orville Wright collection is online and features nearly fifty thousand images, including letters, diaries and notebooks, scrapbooks, drawings, and more.

Access this Web site from http://www.myreportlinks.com

own bike shop. They opened the Wright Cycle Company in 1892. At first, they fixed and sold bicycles. By 1896 Wilbur and Orville were designing their own bicycles as well. Their business was growing and doing well.

The brothers' interest in flying started to grow, too. Wilbur liked to watch birds. He would ride his bike to a place called the Pinnacle in Dayton, Ohio, where he could watch large birds like buzzards and hawks fly and move in the air. Meanwhile, Orville made kites for the neighborhood children. The Wrights thought that gliding through the air would be fun. Orville wrote, "If the bird's wings would sustain it in the air without the use of any muscular effort, we did not see why man could not be sustained by the same means."[1]

In 1896 Otto Lilienthal crashed his glider, which made the brothers more determined to fly. This did not mean just to glide like the birds. They wanted to figure out how they could control flight and make it safe.

TIME TO FLY

The Wrights first experimented with kites. They built a successful biplane box kite that Wilbur controlled with cables. The Wrights needed a place not only with good winds, but also with a soft landing. In August 1900 the Wrights decided that

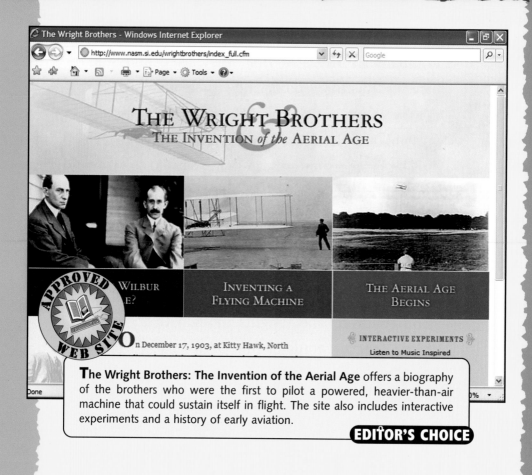

The Wright Brothers: The Invention of the Aerial Age offers a biography of the brothers who were the first to pilot a powered, heavier-than-air machine that could sustain itself in flight. The site also includes interactive experiments and a history of early aviation.

EDITOR'S CHOICE

the sand dunes of Kitty Hawk, North Carolina, would be the best place.

The Wrights experimented with several gliders at Kitty Hawk in 1901. They finally created one that could fly a human. It was balanced and somewhat stable, but it still had problems. The Wrights returned to Dayton and decided to build a wind tunnel to help them study the effects of air movement over and around the plane's design. They would test the shape of wings to see how much lift they got. They also tested wing shapes on bicycles until they came up with just the right wing shape. Soon it was time to go back to Kitty Hawk and test their new and improved glider.

After a few adjustments and hard landings, the Wrights flew their glider. On October 23, 1902, Wilbur glided for 26 seconds and more than 622 feet. Orville wrote, "We now hold all the records! The largest machine . . . the longest time in the air, the smallest angle of descent, and the highest wind."[2]

THE FLYER

Back at Dayton, Ohio, it was time to make a flying machine. The Wright brothers had resolved most of the aeronautic problems. Now they had to add

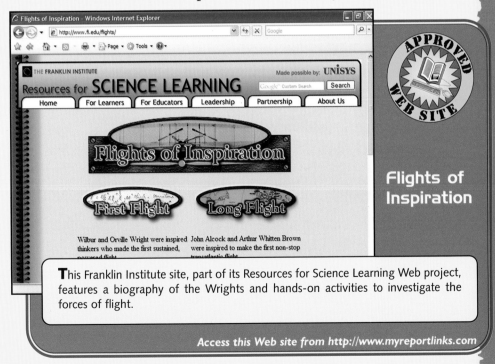

Flights of Inspiration

This Franklin Institute site, part of its Resources for Science Learning Web project, features a biography of the Wrights and hands-on activities to investigate the forces of flight.

Access this Web site from http://www.myreportlinks.com

an engine, which was very heavy. Since they could not find one suitable for their flying machine, they built one. They also built propellers using spruce wood with a laminate finish.

The Wrights were under a lot of pressure. Other inventors, like Samuel Langley, were experimenting with flying machines also. On October 7, 1903, Langley attempted to fly his Aerodrome over the Potomac River, but failed. Now the race was on. The Wrights took the parts of their flying

▲ With Orville Wright at the controls, the dream of flight was truly realized on December 17, 1903.

NOVA | Wright Brothers' Flying Machine | PBS - Windows Internet Explorer

http://www.pbs.org/wgbh/nova/wright/

Page ▾ Tools ▾

PBS HOME   PROGRAMS A–Z   TV SCHEDULES   SUPPORT PBS   SHOP PBS   SEARCH PBS

NOVA SCIENCE PROGRAMMING ON AIR AND ONLINE

SEARCH NOVA

NOVA HOME   TV SCHEDULE   ARCHIVE   ABOUT NOVA   SUBSCRIBE   TEACHERS   RSS   FEEDBACK   TRANSCRIPTS   SHOP NOVA   WATCH NOVA ONLINE   F

Replica of the Wright 1911 Mo

WRIGHT BROTHERS' FLYING MACHINE

Relive the engineering challenges that two bicycle makers overcame to become first in flight.

INTERVIEW & ARTICLE

The Unlikely Inventors
The Smithsonian's Tom Crouch explains why the Wright brothers succeeded where so many others failed

INTERACTIVES & SLIDE SHOW

Pilot the 1903 Flyer
In this clickable illustration of the first airplane, see how the Wright brothers solved the problem of steering

RESOURCES

TV Program Des
Airs on PBS May
Check local listin
may vary.

APPROVED WEB SITE

The **NOVA: Wright Brothers' Flying Machine** site examines the achievements of the Wright brothers, focusing on how they succeeded where so many others had failed. An interactive feature puts readers in the pilot's seat of the 1903 *Flyer*.

machine back to Kitty Hawk and started assembling their plane. Meanwhile, Langley attempted a second flight. His Aerodrome flopped into the river as if the glider were full of concrete. Langley gave up his dream to fly, but the Wright brothers did not.

December 17, 1903, was a windy and bitter day, and the skies billowed with clouds. The brothers hurried to get the plane on a wooden track they had built and into the air. Orville was the pilot. The flying machine sailed down the track at six miles an hour. Moments later, it was airborne. Then it landed gently on the sand. The flight lasted twelve seconds and the flying machine flew 120 feet.

Orville wrote: "This flight . . . was . . . the first in the history of the world in which a machine carrying a man had raised itself by its own power into the air in full flight, had sailed forward without reduction of speed and had finally landed at a point as high as that from which it started."[3]

The two brothers could not stop with just one flight. They flew a second time. Wilbur was the pilot and got the plane to go a little farther—175 feet. The third flight, piloted by Orville, went two hundred feet.

The fourth and final flight of the day was arguably the most dangerous. After lifting off the ground, the flying machine pitched a few hundred feet before Wilbur was able to steady it. The plane flew five hundred feet more before a gust of wind sent it into another roll. Soon the plane was headed for the ground. After 852 feet from its starting point, Wilbur landed. The flight lasted fifty-nine seconds, enough to satisfy the brothers.

BUILDING AN AVIATION COMPANY

The Wrights created a company to sell their airplanes. It was called the Wright Company. Their flying machine was called the *Wright Flyer*.

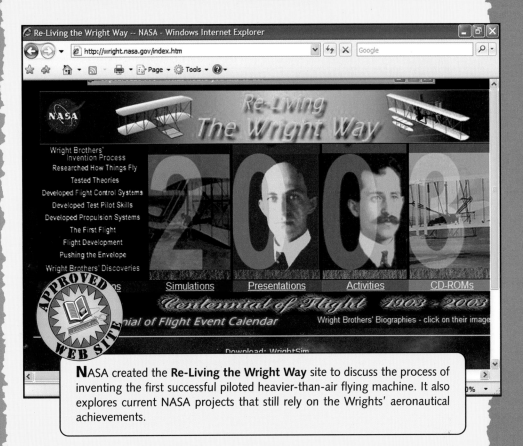

NASA created the **Re-Living the Wright Way** site to discuss the process of inventing the first successful piloted heavier-than-air flying machine. It also explores current NASA projects that still rely on the Wrights' aeronautical achievements.

Although they did well financially, they were continually involved in legal fights to protect their patents. As well, the work took a toll on the men physically and emotionally, especially on Wilbur. In early May 1912 he was diagnosed with typhoid fever. A few weeks later, at the age of forty-five, Wilbur passed away. Orville continued to live out the Wright brothers' legacy, inventing and promoting flight. He remained in the public eye, serving on the National Advisory Committee for Aeronautics (NACA) until his death in 1948.

Bessie Coleman

Opportunities for African Americans in the early twentieth century were not great. People of color often did not have the education or opportunity to work. Racial segregation kept African Americans from attending school and getting good jobs. The thought of becoming a flier or aviator would have been but a passing dream to many young African-American children. Bessie Coleman was born into a large family. She was the tenth out of thirteen siblings. She was born on January 26, 1892, in

Lifeline

1908–1909: Attends the Colored Agricultural and Normal University.

1920: Leaves the United States for France.

1892: Born in Atlanta, Texas, on January 26.

1915: Moves to Chicago.

Chapter 2

Atlanta, Texas. Coleman's parents, Susan and George Coleman, worked as sharecroppers. George was American Indian and Susan was African American.

Coleman had a happy childhood despite the lack of money and racial discrimination. As the older children went to work in the fields with their parents, Coleman assumed responsibilities around the house. She watched her younger siblings and took care of the home. Her free time was spent playing outdoors. Sundays were spent at church.

When Coleman was seven years old her parents separated. Her father felt there were more opportunities to make money in Oklahoma, so he moved to an Indian reservation. Susan Coleman stayed in Texas with her children and continued to work and raise her family.

1922: First air show held at Curtiss Field in New York on September 3.

1995: U.S. Postal Service issues a stamp in Bessie Coleman's honor.

1921: Receives pilot's license on June 15, becoming first African-American licensed pilot in the United States.

1926: Falls to her death in Jacksonville, Florida, on April 30.

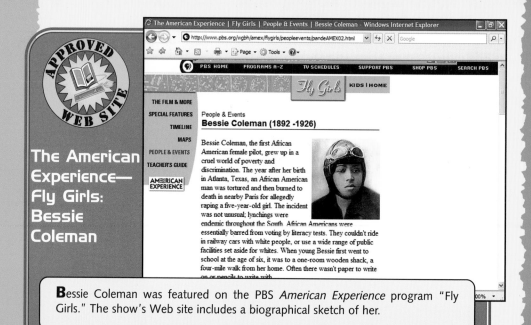

The American Experience— Fly Girls: Bessie Coleman

The American Experience | Fly Girls | People & Events | Bessie Coleman - Windows Internet Explorer

http://www.pbs.org/wgbh/amex/flygirls/peopleevents/pandeAMEX02.html

Google

PBS HOME   PROGRAMS A-Z   TV SCHEDULES   SUPPORT PBS   SHOP PBS   SEARCH PBS

Fly Girls   KIDS | HOME

THE FILM & MORE
SPECIAL FEATURES
TIMELINE
MAPS
PEOPLE & EVENTS
TEACHER'S GUIDE
AMERICAN EXPERIENCE

People & Events
Bessie Coleman (1892 -1926)

Bessie Coleman, the first African American female pilot, grew up in a cruel world of poverty and discrimination. The year after her birth in Atlanta, Texas, an African American man was tortured and then burned to death in nearby Paris for allegedly raping a five-year-old girl. The incident was not unusual; lynchings were endemic throughout the South. African Americans were essentially barred from voting by literacy tests. They couldn't ride in railway cars with white people, or use a wide range of public facilities set aside for whites. When young Bessie first went to school at the age of six, it was to a one-room wooden shack, a four-mile walk from her home. Often there wasn't paper to write on or pencils to write with.

Bessie Coleman was featured on the PBS *American Experience* program "Fly Girls." The show's Web site includes a biographical sketch of her.

Access this Web site from http://www.myreportlinks.com

🧪 SCHOOL DAYS

Education was important to Bessie Coleman and her family. She started school when she was six years old. She walked four miles to a one-room schoolhouse for African-American children. Often Coleman and her fellow students did not have the materials needed to learn properly. Still, Coleman enjoyed school and did well. She loved to read and excelled in math. Even her mother recognized Bessie was gifted in math and had her daughter manage the account books for the family business.

Coleman attended the one-room school through eighth grade, the highest level there. She then graduated from high school, and went on to study at the Colored Agricultural and Normal University (now Langston University) in Langston, Oklahoma. Unfortunately, Coleman did not have the money for all four years. She spent only one semester at the university. While she was at the school, Coleman learned about the Wright Brothers and Harriet Quimby. Quimby was America's first woman pilot to become licensed.

MOVING TO CHICAGO

Hoping for better opportunities, Coleman moved to Chicago in 1915, where she lived with her brother Walter. The big city was exciting and quite different from the dusty agricultural world she had known. Coleman worked as a manicurist for the White Sox barbershop. It was here that she heard fantastic stories from her brother John. He was a World War I veteran who noted that French women were better than American women. "They even fly airplanes," he told her.[1]

That was exactly what Coleman needed to hear. She dreamed of making something of her life, and becoming a pilot seemed like a fun and lofty ambition. There was a huge problem, though. Women had a difficult time getting anyone to teach them to fly. Aviation was considered a man's hobby. Being African American and a woman only made this harder for Coleman. She could not find anyone who would teach her to fly.

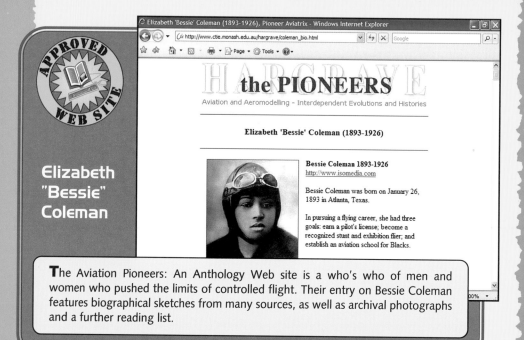

Elizabeth "Bessie" Coleman

Elizabeth 'Bessie' Coleman (1893-1926), Pioneer Aviatrix - Windows Internet Explorer

http://www.ctie.monash.edu.au/hargrave/coleman_bio.html

Google

the PIONEERS

Aviation and Aeromodelling - Interdependent Evolutions and Histories

Elizabeth 'Bessie' Coleman (1893-1926)

Bessie Coleman 1893-1926
http://www.isomedia.com

Bessie Coleman was born on January 26, 1893 in Atlanta, Texas.

In pursuing a flying career, she had three goals: earn a pilot's license; become a recognized stunt and exhibition flier; and establish an aviation school for Blacks.

The Aviation Pioneers: An Anthology Web site is a who's who of men and women who pushed the limits of controlled flight. Their entry on Bessie Coleman features biographical sketches from many sources, as well as archival photographs and a further reading list.

Access this Web site from http://www.myreportlinks.com

France seemed to be the best place for Coleman to go. France was more tolerant toward women and people of color. With help, she raised enough money to travel to France and take flying lessons.

FLYING WITH THE FRENCH

In November 1920 Coleman left for France. She was excited about her new venture. She enrolled in the School of Aviation of Freres Caudron at Le Crotoy in Somme, France. She flew in a French plane called the Nieuport Type 82, and finished the ten-course program in seven months. Coleman learned some dangerous moves in the airplane, including tailspins, banking, and looping the loop.

On June 15, 1921, the prestigious Federation Aeronautique Internationale (FAI) granted Coleman her pilot's license. Though Coleman was not the first black woman to receive a license from the FAI, she was the first American to receive a license from the French school. Moreover, she became the first licensed black pilot in the United States. Coleman spent three more months studying in France before returning to the United States.

Coleman wanted to become a show aviator and fly the skies as a stuntwoman. The young pilot soon realized that to do this she needed more training. Coleman headed back to France. In August 1922 she returned to the United States with a new image in mind.

QUEEN BESS

Bessie Coleman had her first air show on September 3, 1922, at Curtiss Field near New York City. The show featured Coleman as "the world's greatest woman flyer!" She also flew in other shows in Memphis, Chicago, and Texas. Her daredevil flying awed spectators. Both white- and black-run newspapers raved about Bessie. Her fans called her Queen Bess or Brave Bessie.

Coleman was on her way to becoming not just a celebrity, but also a movie star. She moved to southern California to act in a movie for an African-American film company. After learning she

The Curtiss JN-4 Jenny was used to train pilots in World War I. They were later sold to the public and widely used by daring pilots like Bessie Coleman.

was to play the role of a poor African-American girl who moved to the city, Coleman broke her contract. She felt it was degrading to women. She went back to flying, which truly was her first love. She also had dreams of opening an aviation school.

COLEMAN'S DREAM CRASHES

Coleman needed only a plane to open an aviation school. While in Los Angeles, an advertising executive with a tire company told Coleman he would buy her a plane if she dropped leaflets advertising his company. Coleman agreed and he gave her a JN-4 "Jenny" airplane. It was an army surplus trainer plane. Unfortunately, on the first flight it stalled and crashed with Coleman in it. She survived but suffered a broken leg. She could not fly for four months. She sent a message to her fans, who were relieved that she was okay, but sad that she had to cancel any forthcoming air shows. She said, "Tell them all that as soon as I can walk I'm going to fly!"[2]

When Coleman's leg was better, she returned to Chicago. Without any money, a job, or a plane, it was difficult to do what she wanted—open a flight school for African-American aviators. She opened an office in Chicago, but had to return to stunt flying to earn money.

Bessie Coleman headed back to her roots in Texas. For pay, she gave lectures and showed films of her flights—mostly to small church groups, theaters, and all-black public schools. She also organized air shows with borrowed planes and traveled to Florida and Georgia. At her air shows, Coleman refused to have segregated seating and refused to fly if not everyone entered through the same gate. "I wasn't going to let them humiliate my people, who were coming to see me. I told them I would not fly until they let the blacks through the same gate as the whites."[3]

Soon, Bessie Coleman had enough money to buy her own plane. It was another old Curtiss Jenny. A young white aviator, William Wills, flew the plane from Texas and met Coleman in Florida. While in Florida, Coleman also opened a beauty shop to help raise more money. She had her heart set on opening an all-black flying school.

🧪 Disaster in the Air

William Wills had problems flying the plane from Texas to Florida. He had to make several stops. One mechanic commented that he was surprised Wills had even flown it so far. But Coleman had a performance on May 1, 1926, for a May Day celebration, and the plane needed to be at the airfield and ready for flight. It was the end of April and things were going well for Bessie Coleman.

The evening before her show, Coleman and Wills took the Curtiss Jenny up for a test run. Wills was piloting the plane. During a planned dive, the plane suddenly lost control and went into a tailspin, flinging Coleman out of the plane. She was not wearing her safety belt or a parachute. Coleman fell almost a mile to her death. Even though Wills wore a seat belt, he died when the plane crashed.

Thousands of people attended Coleman's funeral in Orlando, Florida. Her body was taken by train to Chicago, where she was buried. She was just thirty-four years old.

FULFILLING COLEMAN'S DREAM

Bessie Coleman was one of the most respected aviators of her day. She refused to cave under the

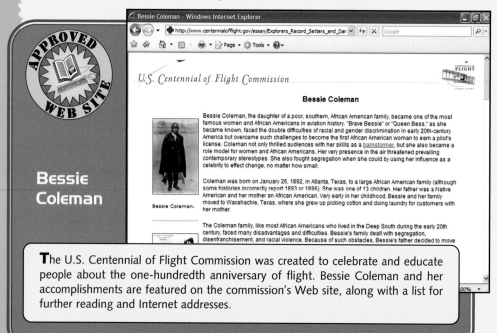

Bessie Coleman

The U.S. Centennial of Flight Commission was created to celebrate and educate people about the one-hundredth anniversary of flight. Bessie Coleman and her accomplishments are featured on the commission's Web site, along with a list for further reading and Internet addresses.

Access this Web site from http://www.myreportlinks.com

pressures of society and dreamed big dreams. In a day when many were against her race, Coleman defeated all odds. She loved flying and felt that "the air is the only place free from prejudices."[4]

At the time of Coleman's death, she had raised almost enough money to open her all-black flying school. She once said, "I decided blacks should not have to experience the difficulties I had faced so I decided to open a flying school and teach other black women to fly."[5]

She would never see it happen, but others continued her legacy. In 1929 William Powell, author of *Black Wings*, established the Bessie Coleman Aero Club in Los Angeles, California. Her example also inspired many African-American aviators to pursue their dreams of flight, including the Blackbirds, the Black Hobos, the Tuskegee Airmen, and Willa Brown.

Years later, Bessie Coleman is still acknowledged for her courage. In 1992 the city of Chicago declared May 2 Bessie Coleman Day. Three years later, the U.S. Postal Service issued a Bessie Coleman stamp honoring "her singular accomplishment in becoming the world's first African American pilot and, by definition, an American legend."[6]

Charles Lindbergh

In the early twentieth century, young men and women around the country dreamed of flying. To become an aviator was not only heroic, but it also seemed like a glamorous life. To a young boy in Little Falls, Minnesota, seeing an airplane fly over his home was more excitement than he could stand. Charles Augustus Lindbergh knew early on that he wanted to fly. He remembered:

Lifeline

1922: Enrolls in the Nebraska Aircraft Corporation School of Flying.

1927: Pilots the Spirit of St. Louis *from San Diego to New York, May 10–11, setting transcontinental record.*

1902: Born in Detroit, Michigan, on February 4.

1926: Begins flying for the airmail service.

One day, before the first World War began, . . . I heard an unusually loud engine noise. I ran to the window and climbed out onto the roof. There was an airplane flying upriver, below the treetops on the banks. I learned that it was carrying passengers from a field near Little Falls. Of course I wanted to fly in it, but my mother said that it would be much too expensive and dangerous.[1]

🧪 GROWING UP

Charles Lindbergh was born in Detroit, Michigan, on February 4, 1902. He was raised in Little Falls, Minnesota, on a 110-acre farm. Charles Augustus Lindbergh, Sr., was a lawyer and then a congressman for Minnesota. His mother, Evangeline Land Lindbergh, was a chemistry teacher. She had graduated from the University of Michigan. Charles Lindbergh

1929: Marries Anne Morrow.

1974: Dies of lymphatic cancer on August 26.

1927: Becomes first man to fly solo across the Atlantic Ocean, from Long Island, New York, to Paris, France, May 20–21.

1932: Firstborn son is kidnapped and murdered.

spent his time between his home in Minnesota and Washington, D.C., where his father lived during his terms as congressman.

Lindbergh loved the outdoors. He also enjoyed mechanics and science. As a young boy, his father taught him how to hunt. When he was eleven, Lindbergh learned to drive the family car. At fourteen, he spent time with his father on campaign tours. By sixteen, Lindbergh was running the family farm. Because of his knowledge in mechanics, he could keep the machines in good form.

FANCIES OF FLIGHT

Lindbergh's interest in flying was first aroused at just nine

Lindbergh was a barnstormer and flew in the air mail service. Both were dangerous jobs that may have helped him prepare to fly across the Atlantic.

years old, when he saw a plane fly over the farm. It was a barnstormer. Barnstormers were pilots who performed stunts and often raced in planes. Later, Lindbergh grew more excited about flying when he went to an air show in Virginia.

When it was time to choose a college, Lindbergh wanted to attend the Massachusetts

Institute of Technology (MIT). This school had a new program in aeronautical engineering. Unfortunately, Lindbergh's grades were not good enough to get into MIT. Instead, he attended the University of Wisconsin. Still, his heart was not in his studies. He dreamed of being a pilot. After just a year and a half of college, he dropped out.

THE DAREDEVIL

Lindbergh decided to enroll in the Nebraska Aircraft Corporation School of Flying in April 1922. He paid five hundred dollars, but soon discovered it was not a good school. He was the only student. His instructor, Ira Biffle, did not seem to care much about teaching. Lindbergh flew only eight hours over a six-week period.

Luckily, Lindbergh's time and money were not entirely wasted in Nebraska. While there, he met a barnstormer named Erold Bahl. Lindbergh convinced Bahl to let him go with him on his barnstorming tour. Together they flew from town to town, putting on shows and taking people up in the plane for a fee.

During this time, Lindbergh learned how to perform many stunts. Among the stunts learned was wing walking, or walking across the plane's wings while in the air.

A young mechanic named Pete taught Lindbergh the tricks of the trade. Lindbergh wrote:

The life of aviation hero Charles A. Lindbergh is examined in the site **The American Experience—Lindbergh**. Learn more about the famous *Spirit of St. Louis*, the plane that carried Lindbergh on his flight from New York to Paris, as well as the tragic story of his son's kidnapping and murder.

EDITOR'S CHOICE

. . . It was from him [Pete] I learned that a wing walker didn't really hang by his teeth from a leather strap attached to the landing gear's spreader bar. He simply held the strap in his mouth while his weight was safely supported by a steel cable hooked to a strong harness underneath his coat. The cable was too thin for eyes on the ground to see and the effect on the crowd was as good as though none were there.[2]

As a child, Lindbergh had a fear of falling from high places. It is amazing that he was able to overcome this fear and walk on a wing of an airplane hundreds of feet in the air. Charles Lindbergh became known as Daredevil Lindbergh. "People came for miles to watch me climb back and forth over wings, and finally leap off into space."[3]

DELIVERING THE MAIL

Still, after a year of barnstorming, Lindbergh had not flown solo. In April 1923 he bought his first plane. It was a World War I Curtiss JN-4 "Jenny." He was not an experienced flyer and nearly crashed on several occasions. He soon realized that a life in barnstorming was not just extremely dangerous, it also did not pay well.

Lindbergh enlisted as an aviation cadet in the United States Army in January 1924. He not only learned how to fly, he also learned radio, photography, maintenance, meteorology, and navigation—all important things to know. It was here that Lindbergh thrived. He was motivated to do well and was serious about learning to fly. He knew that this training would take him far. He thought that ". . . an Air Service pilot's wings were like a silver passport to the realm of light."[4]

Lindbergh worked at one of the most dangerous jobs—airmail service. It was operated by the United States Post Office. This service had been around since 1918. Statistics show that thirty-one of the first forty pilots hired were killed in crashes.[5] Routes took flyers from New York City to San Francisco, St. Louis, and Chicago, and other places in between.

Lindbergh worked in St. Louis, Missouri, with Robinson Aircraft Corporation. He became their chief pilot. Lindbergh and the pilots under him did very well. They had few crashes. When they did crash-land, they were often able to save their plane. They were also known for delivering the mail on time.

While Lindbergh was delivering mail, he heard about a contest. It was called the Orteig Prize. Twenty-five thousand dollars would be awarded to the first aviator to fly nonstop from New York to Paris, or vice versa. Lindbergh now had a new goal to reach.

GOING FOR THE PRIZE

Lindbergh wanted to be the first to fly across the Atlantic. But he needed money to buy a plane capable of carrying him overseas in one hop. A group of businessmen offered to help. A small aircraft company in San Diego called Ryan Aircraft built a plane for Lindbergh in sixty days. It cost $10,580. When it was completed on April 26, 1927, the plane was christened the *Spirit of St. Louis*.

To fly nonstop across the Atlantic Ocean, the *Spirit of St. Louis* needed a big gas tank. A container was put in front of his seat, but that

▲ *Charles Lindbergh poses in front of the* Spirit of St. Louis. *He was the first to successfully fly across the Atlantic Ocean, over 3,610 miles, becoming an international star.*

blocked Lindbergh's view. He did not mind the fact that he could not see directly out the front window, though. "There's not much need to see ahead in normal flight. . . . All I need is a window on each side to see through . . ."[6] The wingspan was also longer than normal to help support the additional load of the gas tank. To cut down on weight, Lindbergh decided not to bring essential items with him. This included a radio and a parachute. He did bring a compass, five sandwiches, a gallon of water, and a chart.

On May 10, 1927, as Lindbergh was leaving San Diego for New York, a report came in that two pilots had taken off from Paris, straight for New York. Suddenly, Lindbergh's dream to win the Orteig Prize seemed to be gone, but not for long. The pilots had been seen over the Atlantic, but they were never heard from again. Lindbergh was back in the race to become the first person to cross the Atlantic nonstop. On May 12, he flew from San Diego to Roosevelt Field in New York to prepare for his long journey. The trip broke the existing transcontinental flight record.

THE JOURNEY ACROSS THE ATLANTIC

On May 20, 1927, at 7:54 in the morning, like a silver bullet the *Spirit of St. Louis* took off from Roosevelt Field. Glad to be flying alone, Lindbergh only had himself and the plane to worry about.

41

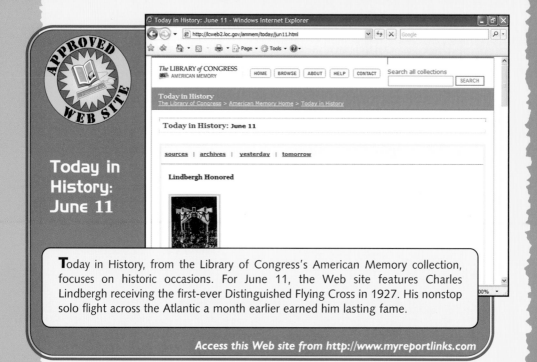

Today in History: June 11

Today in History, from the Library of Congress's American Memory collection, focuses on historic occasions. For June 11, the Web site features Charles Lindbergh receiving the first-ever Distinguished Flying Cross in 1927. His nonstop solo flight across the Atlantic a month earlier earned him lasting fame.

Access this Web site from http://www.myreportlinks.com

However, he had a long journey ahead. Lindbergh flew up the northeast coast and was seen flying over Nova Scotia and Newfoundland. From there, he began his flight across the Atlantic. He dealt with fog, ice, and sleep deprivation. He saw icebergs and flew high to avoid them. Ice covered his wings, which could cause him to crash. "That worried me a great deal and I debated whether I should keep on or go back. I decided I must not think any more about going back."[7]

After eighteen hours, Lindbergh was only halfway to his destination and without a pinch of land in sight. It was hard to stay awake. Shaking his head and tensing his muscles helped. The next time he saw land, nine hours later, he was over Ireland.

Around 9:52, local French time, in the evening on May 21, Lindbergh spotted the Eiffel Tower. Soon Le Bourget Airport was sighted and he safely landed. Dozens of people were there to greet him. It was a frenzy as people grabbed him and started to rip apart his plane. Some people wanted a souvenir. Charles Lindbergh had flown 3,610 miles in thirty-three hours; he had won the Orteig Prize. He was quickly known around the world and became America's biggest celebrity. President Calvin Coolidge gave him the Distinguished Flying Cross. Congress gave him a Medal of Honor. In reaction to all the attention, Lindbergh said, "I was astonished at the effect my successful landing in France had on the nations of the world. To me, it was like a match lighting a bonfire."[8]

LATER YEARS

In 1929 Lindbergh married Anne Morrow. She was the daughter of Ambassador Dwight Morrow. Shortly after their marriage, they had a son, Charles Lindbergh III. Sadly, hard times fell on the Lindberghs. Charles III was kidnapped and killed. The media attention caused the Lindberghs to leave the country and live in Europe.

The achievements of aviation pioneer Charles A. Lindbergh are recounted on this Web page from the U.S. Centennial of Flight Commission. Their celebration of one hundred years of flight includes archival photographs of Lindbergh and the *Spirit of St. Louis.*

Access this Web site from http://www.myreportlinks.com

Charles Lindbergh and his family returned to the United States in 1939. World War II had broken out in Europe and Lindbergh was an outspoken opponent to any American involvement. But after the Japanese attacked Pearl Harbor on December 7, 1941, and the United States entered the war, Lindbergh changed his position. In 1944 he served as a civilian advisor to the United States Army and Navy in the Pacific. He participated in fifty combat missions and helped improve the technical performance of American fighter planes.[9]

After the war, Lindbergh spent the remainder of his years in conservation. He campaigned for forest preservation, the protection of endangered animal species and marine life, and in defense of primitive tribes. Charles Lindbergh passed away on August 26, 1974, of the cancer lymphoma. In 1997 the Lindbergh Foundation was started in honor of Charles Lindbergh and his brave vision that launched the world into transcontinental flight.

Amelia Earhart

When she was growing up, Amelia Earhart was a typical tomboy. Much to her grandmother's dismay, Amelia preferred the outdoors and activities such as hopping fences to sitting inside. As a young girl, Earhart showed an interest in learning to fly. In a nature poem she wrote as a young girl she inscribed,

Lifeline

1921: Begins flying lessons with Neta Snook.

1931: Marries George Putnam.

1897: Born in Atchison, Kansas, July 24.

1928: First woman to fly across the Atlantic Ocean, June 17–18.

I watch the birds flying all day long
And I want to fly too.
Don't they look down sometimes, I wonder,
And wish they were me
When I'm going to the circus with my daddy?[1]

CHILDHOOD

Earhart was born on July 24, 1897. Her parents were Amy Otis and Edwin Stanton Earhart. Amelia was born at her mother's parents' home in Atchison, Kansas. This is where she and her younger sister, Grace Muriel, would spend much of their childhood.

Amelia's mother came from a well-to-do home. Her father did not. Edwin Earhart struggled to become a lawyer and made some bad business decisions that caused the family financial problems.

Amelia Earhart liked to work with her hands building things. After visiting the World's Fair in 1904 in St. Louis, Missouri, Earhart became fascinated with the roller

1932: First woman to fly solo nonstop from coast to coast, August 24–25.

1937: Begins flight around the world on June 1. Contact lost on July 2; largest air and sea search in naval history begins. Search called off on July 19.

1932: First woman to fly solo across the Atlantic, May 20–21.

Amelia Earhart Birthplace Museum - Windows Internet Explorer

http://www.ameliaearhartmuseum.org/   Google

Page ▾ Tools ▾

Amelia Earhart Birthplace Museum
223 North Terrace Street
Atchison, KS 66002
(913) 367-4217
www.ameliaearhartbirthplacemuseum.org

Home
Museum
Other Attractions
Amelia Earhart
Ninety Nines
Sponsors
Trustees/Volunteers
Related Links

The Atchison, Kansas, home where Amelia Earhart was born, in 1897, is now a museum celebrating the life of the pioneering aviator. Learn more about Earhart and the influence her achievements have had on women pilots ever since at the **Amelia Earhart Birthplace Museum** site.

EDITOR'S CHOICE

coaster. But her mother refused to let her ride it. When she got home, Earhart, her sister, and an uncle built their own small version of a roller coaster. It was a wood box with roller-skate wheels that sat on some planks that were greased with lard. Earhart took the first ride down, crash-landing. "The car and passenger tipped over at the edge of the roof but the excited passenger claimed, 'It's just like flying.'"[2] Earhart would not let this fall stop her from trying again. She added some more track and soon the roller coaster worked.

In 1905, when Earhart was eight years old, she and Grace were sent to their grandparents' home to live. Her father's law practice had failed, and her parents decided to move to Des Moines, Iowa, to start anew. The sisters ended up spending three years with their grandparents.

Earhart was a bright child. She was independent and did not like to be told she could not do something because she was a girl. Girls did not play team sports in school at this time, but Earhart wanted to play basketball. She approached the team captain during a practice and blurted out, "We girls would like to play."[3] He agreed to teach her some moves. Earhart taught some friends and soon they were playing basketball for fun.

When Earhart was not playing, she loved to read and write poetry. She could memorize stories and tell them to her friends. This love for writing would have her complete two books later in life.

FIRST SIGHTING

In 1908 the Earhart sisters moved to Des Moines to live with their parents. It was at the Iowa State Fair when Earhart was ten years old that she saw her first plane. It was just a few years after the Wright brothers had created a powered flying machine. People had a great interest in airplanes. Yet, the plane Earhart saw did not leave a good impression on her. "It was a thing of rusty wire and wood and looked not at all interesting," she recalled.[4]

After graduating from high school, college was in Earhart's sights. With no idea about what she wanted to do, Earhart attended the Ogontz School in Rydal, Pennsylvania. She did well and was active in school activities.

LOVE FOR FLYING GROWS

In 1918 Earhart visited her sister in Toronto, Canada. World War I had been going on for four years and many soldiers were in the streets returning from the war in Europe. Earhart wanted to help, so she took a Red Cross first aid class and

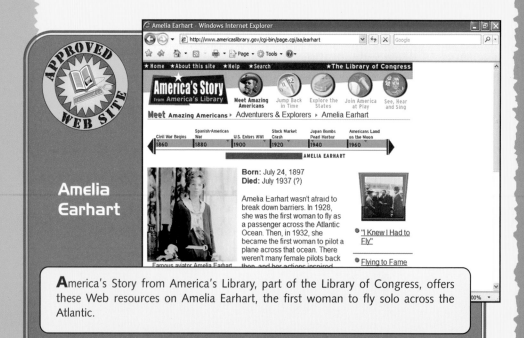

Amelia
Earhart

America's Story from America's Library, part of the Library of Congress, offers these Web resources on Amelia Earhart, the first woman to fly solo across the Atlantic.

Access this Web site from http://www.myreportlinks.com

signed up for the Volunteers Aid Detachment. At a hospital in Canada, Earhart emptied bedpans, scrubbed floors, and cared for injured soldiers.

Her interest in airplanes grew as well. She met a colonel at the stables who invited her to an airfield. Planes had changed a lot by this time and to Earhart they were beautiful. "They were full-sized birds that slid on the hard-packed snow and rose into the air with an extra roar that echoed from the evergreens that banked the edge of the field."[5]

Earhart was hooked. She wanted to fly, but no one would let her. The next best thing was talking to the pilots and being around the planes as much as she could. At the Toronto Exposition, she saw a pilot doing loops in the air. The pilot began to dive at the crowd, sending people running. Earhart stood her ground. "I remember the mingled fear and pleasure which surged over me as I watched that small plane at the top of its earthward swoop. . . . I believe that little red airplane said something to me as it swished by."[6]

TIME TO FLY SOLO

Earhart moved with her family to Los Angeles, California. She attended another air show at Dougherty Field and finally had her first airplane ride. She realized that learning to fly was not cheap. She took a job at a local telephone company to pay for her lessons. Her instructor was

Neta Snook, the first woman to graduate from the Curtiss School of Aviation. Earhart first learned all about the plane she was flying. She then decided to do some stunt training before she attempted to fly solo. She learned to loop, dive, and fly upside down. Soon, it was time for Earhart to fly solo. She was scared not of flying, but of landing. During her first solo flight, Earhart climbed to

▲ Earhart checks equipment in her plane before one of her many record-setting flights.

five thousand feet. She looped around and then landed. It was not a good landing, but Earhart was now one of only a few licensed female pilots. All she needed was a plane of her own.

MAKING FIRSTS

Earhart bought her first plane for two thousand dollars. She participated in air shows and tried to make a living flying but found it difficult. She moved to New York City and took a job teaching immigrants about United States culture and how to speak English. There, she heard about two men who were going to attempt a flight across the Atlantic Ocean. Charles Lindbergh already had done it the year before. The woman who was paying for the flight Earhart was interested in was wealthy, and she wanted a woman to be part of the crew. Earhart got the job, although she would only be a passenger. On June 18, 1928, the plane, *Friendship*, landed safely at Burry Port in Wales, England, and Earhart made history. It took forty hours and twenty minutes to cross the Atlantic.

Upon their arrival back in the states, Earhart was surprised by all the attention she received. After all, she did not pilot the plane. She wrote a book about the experience titled *Forty Hours and Twenty Minutes*. Despite the attention, Earhart wanted to make headlines herself, not as a passenger but as a pilot.

53

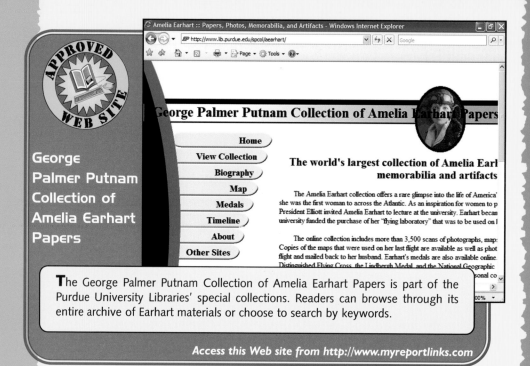

APPROVED WEB SITE

George Palmer Putnam Collection of Amelia Earhart Papers

George Palmer Putnam Collection of Amelia Earhart Papers

The world's largest collection of Amelia Earhart memorabilia and artifacts

The Amelia Earhart collection offers a rare glimpse into the life of America's she was the first woman to across the Atlantic. As an inspiration for women to p President Elliott invited Amelia Earhart to lecture at the university. Earhart becam university funded the purchase of her "flying laboratory" that was to be used on l

The online collection includes more than 3,500 scans of photographs, maps Copies of the maps that were used on her last flight are available as well as phot flight and mailed back to her husband. Earhart's medals are also available online. Distinguished Flying Cross, the Lindbergh Medal, and the National Geographic

Home
View Collection
Biography
Map
Medals
Timeline
About
Other Sites

The George Palmer Putnam Collection of Amelia Earhart Papers is part of the Purdue University Libraries' special collections. Readers can browse through its entire archive of Earhart materials or choose to search by keywords.

Access this Web site from http://www.myreportlinks.com

Earhart broke cross-country records over the United States and became the first woman to fly across the continent and back again. In 1930 she broke the altitude record for autogiros (helicopter-like crafts), flying to 18,415 feet. It was easy now for Earhart to get jobs. She was in great demand.

In 1931 Amelia Earhart married publisher George Palmer Putnam. He had helped select her for the flight across the Atlantic on *Friendship*.

LADY LINDY

In 1932 Earhart became the first woman to fly across the Atlantic Ocean alone. Her goal was to leave on May 20, the same day Charles Lindbergh left, and arrive in Paris. It was exactly five years after Charles Lindbergh made the historic flight.

Unlike Lindbergh's flight, Earhart had problems. A storm that was thought to be farther south came in her direction. She had winds pushing against her, slowing her pace. When she turned on the reserve gasoline tank, it was defective. Gasoline ran down her neck. Finally, she spotted land. It was Ireland. She was on course but had to stop before anything else went wrong. Instead of landing in France, she landed in Ireland. Now she was the first woman to cross the Atlantic, not once, but twice. When she returned to the United States, she was honored with medals, receptions, and parades. Earhart became known as "Lady Lindy." Not only was she an aviator like Charles Lindbergh, but she looked a lot like him, too.

Earhart toured the country talking about her adventure. She also wrote articles for women's magazines. On January 11, 1935, she broke another record. She became the first person to fly from Honolulu, Hawaii, to Oakland, California.

A NEW RECORD IN MIND

It takes weeks to plan a trip around the world, especially when no one has done it before. Earhart wanted to be the first but knew she could not make the trip alone. She decided to have four

55

people on board, including herself. Harry Manning, captain of the USS *President Roosevelt*, had taught her much about navigation. He would be the navigator. Paul Mantz would be the technical advisor, and Fred Noonan would be the second navigator. Earhart was confident she could do this, but her husband was not. Putnam tried to talk her out of it.

During a press conference on February 11, 1937, Earhart announced to the world her plans. Originally, her crew would make the journey from west to east. They would take off from Hawaii and cross the Pacific. However, the flight was postponed on March 19, 1937, after a failed attempt to leave the island greatly damaged the plane. While the plane was being repaired, Earhart changed the direction of the course to avoid monsoon season in Africa. The crew—now down to just Earhart and Noonan—would instead be flying east to west. She intended to fly as close to the equator as possible. The last leg of her flight would be over the vast Pacific Ocean, perhaps the most dangerous part of the trip because there are so few places to land.

AROUND THE WORLD

On June 1, 1937, Earhart and Noonan took off on the first leg of the journey. They flew from Miami to Puerto Rico. From there they would travel to

South America, then across to Africa, and east to Pakistan. Australia and New Guinea would be the next two visits. They would fly to a tiny island called Howland Island. This island would be a refueling stop. Then they would fly on to Honolulu, Hawaii, and back home to Oakland, California.

▲ Amelia Earhart and navigator Fred Noonan climb into the Lockheed Electra L-10E during their flight around the world. After completing about twenty-two thousand miles of the journey, contact was lost on July 2, 1937.

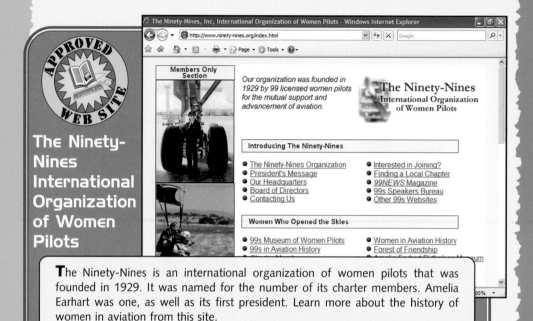

The Ninety-Nines International Organization of Women Pilots

Our organization was founded in 1929 by 99 licensed women pilots for the mutual support and advancement of aviation.

The Ninety-Nines
International Organization
of Women Pilots

Introducing The Ninety-Nines

- The Ninety-Nines Organization
- President's Message
- Our Headquarters
- Board of Directors
- Contacting Us

- Interested in Joining?
- Finding a Local Chapter
- *99NEWS* Magazine
- 99s Speakers Bureau
- Other 99s Websites

Women Who Opened the Skies

- 99s Museum of Women Pilots
- 99s in Aviation History

- Women in Aviation History
- Forest of Friendship

The Ninety-Nines is an international organization of women pilots that was founded in 1929. It was named for the number of its charter members. Amelia Earhart was one, as well as its first president. Learn more about the history of women in aviation from this site.

Access this Web site from http://www.myreportlinks.com

The trip was going well. Earhart and Noonan traveled over five continents. At each stop they enjoyed the culture and exotic food. They took camel rides in Karachi, Pakistan. She telephoned her husband from Karachi and told him she was "Swell. Never better!"[7]

FINAL DESTINATION BECOMES A MYSTERY

But fun times were not to last. Earhart had flown almost all the way around the world and was on her last stretch. She was on schedule, too. Because Howland Island was so small, a white-painted ship named *Itasca* sent up a plume of black smoke at the estimated time of Earhart's arrival. This was a signal to Earhart and Noonan that they were at Howland Island. The ship had made some contact with Earhart, but the radio frequency was scratchy. Earhart was off course, but by how much, no one was certain. In one of her last radio transmissions Earhart said, "We must be on you but cannot see you but gas is running low have been unable [to] reach you by radio we are flying at 1000 feet."[8] By this time, she was two hours over her intended schedule and needed to land.

The last message came in a little over an hour later. Earhart was not heard from again. It was July 2, 1937. A great search and rescue was put in place. The *Itasca*, a battleship, four destroyers, a minesweeper, and an aircraft carrier searched for the lost plane for sixteen days. Nothing was ever recovered.

Amelia Earhart not only set new aviation records, but she also changed how the world viewed women. Her legacy has empowered women to try new things, to have courage, and to not let gender keep them from following their dreams.

Benjamin O. Davis, Jr.

On July 1, 1932, Benjamin Davis, Jr., entered his room at West Point Academy in New York. The room had two beds, but unlike the other cadets, he did not have a roommate. Davis had spent much of his time daydreaming about how wonderful the next four years at West Point would be. Davis could hardly wait to start his training at the academy. While he wanted to serve his country just like his father had, most of all he wanted to fly.

A few days after his arrival, Davis's

Lifeline

1932–1936: Attends the United States Military Academy, West Point, N.Y.

1941: Reports to Flying School at Tuskegee Army Air Field.

1912: Born in Washington, D.C., on December 18.

1936: Marries Agatha Scott.

life changed drastically. He overheard a conversation among his fellow cadets in the bathroom. They decided that they did not want anything to do with Davis because he was an African American. From that moment on, Davis became an invisible man at West Point. Although everyone at the academy denied that Davis had been silenced—meaning no one would talk or have anything to do with him—it was clear that his presence was not welcome.

Davis ate alone. He roomed alone. On the bus, no one would sit with him. No one talked to Davis unless he had to out of duty. Davis wrote, "The cruel treatment was designed to make me buckle, but I refused to buckle in any way. I maintained my self-respect . . . I continued to hold my head up high."[1]

The United States military in its earlier years was segregated. The African-American

1943: Takes command of 332nd Fighter Group.

1970: Retires from Air Force.

2002: Dies at Walter Reed Army Medical Center, Washington, D.C., on July 4.

1942: Takes command of 99th Fighter Squadron.

1954: Promoted to Brigadier General, becoming first African American to hold the rank.

1998: Promoted to General (Retired).

men who joined were put into their own, all-black units, often commanded by a white person. As Davis continued his training, he became more aware of this problem and decided he would one day change it.

EARLY YEARS

Davis, Jr., was born on December 18, 1912. At the time of his birth, his father, Benjamin Davis, Sr., was a first lieutenant of cavalry at Fort D. A. Russell in Wyoming. Davis's mother, Elnora, wanted to have her baby back in Washington at her in-laws' home. She traveled from Wyoming to Washington with her first daughter, Olive. There she had Benjamin O. Davis, Jr., and then returned to Wyoming.

Davis looked up to his father. He was in the Army, but because of the color of his skin, he did not have an easy time. Still, Davis, Sr., stood up for what he believed, and this attitude set a great example for his son. "How lucky I was to have a father who, in spite of formidable obstacles, would fight for his beliefs and ambitions and win!" explained Davis.[2]

NOT ALL BAD CHILDHOOD

On February 9, 1916, just nine days after the birth of his second sister, Elnora, Benjamin's mother died. Davis did not remember much about her

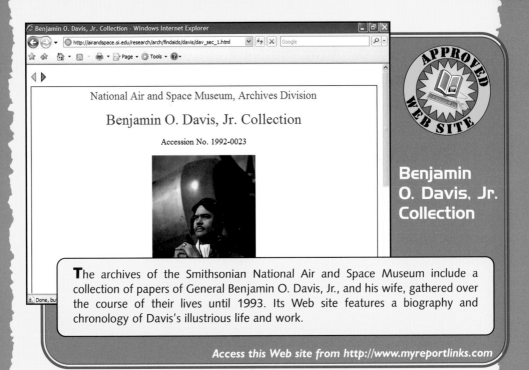

National Air and Space Museum, Archives Division

Benjamin O. Davis, Jr. Collection

Accession No. 1992-0023

Benjamin O. Davis, Jr. Collection

The archives of the Smithsonian National Air and Space Museum include a collection of papers of General Benjamin O. Davis, Jr., and his wife, gathered over the course of their lives until 1993. Its Web site features a biography and chronology of Davis's illustrious life and work.

Access this Web site from http://www.myreportlinks.com

except what he was told. He was just four years old. Davis's father was stationed in the Philippines at the time, so the three children were sent to live with their grandparents in Washington, D.C.

Davis's first job as a young boy was as a newspaper carrier. He helped deliver the *Evening Star*. Davis would load up his cart with neatly folded papers and deliver them to neighbors. He also attended school in 1918 and 1919. They were all-black schools and, in Davis's opinion, provided an outstanding education.

Soon he and his siblings were reunited with their father, who had remarried by this time. They moved to Tuskegee Institute, an all-black school in

Alabama. According to Davis, this school was where the Army sent black officers when they did not know what to do with them. Still, people like Davis's father worked hard to educate the young men who were sent here so that they could go back into their communities, both skilled in trades and educated.

Davis attended a small elementary school at the Tuskegee Institute called the Children's House. He did well and pursued other activities like piano, trumpet lessons, and baseball.

DREAMS OF FLYING

Davis's father was transferred to Cleveland, Ohio, in July 1924. During the summer months while his parents toured Europe, Davis visited his Uncle Ernest's farm back in Washington, D.C. During the summer of 1926, he saw his first barnstormer put on a show at Bolling Air Field. Davis loved watching the plane maneuver in the air. On a second visit, he paid five dollars to go for a ride. Davis did not remember it well. Flying in an open cockpit was overwhelming. He had goggles and a helmet on but felt the airplane was frail.

Even so, Davis had a desire to become an aviator. Charles Lindbergh's flight across the Atlantic in 1927 inspired Davis further, and he read everything he could about Lindbergh.

🔙🔜 ▾ http://www.centennialofflight.gov/essay/Dictionary/DAVIS/DI184.htm ▾ ✦✦ ✕ Google 🔎 ▾

U.S. Centennial of Flight Commission

Benjamin O. Davis, Jr.

Lt. Gen. Benjamin O. Davis
US

The **U.S. Centennial of Flight Commission: Benjamin O. Davis, Jr.,** formed to commemorate the one-hundredth anniversary of the Wright brothers' 1903 flight, features a brief biography of General Benjamin O. Davis, Jr., on its Web site.

Davis graduated from Central High in 1929. He was president of the student council and graduated top of his class. He enrolled in Western Reserve University in Cleveland. School frustrated Davis. His thoughts were still on flying. Yet, becoming a pilot was almost impossible for a black man during that time. There was an opportunity, however, for Davis to attend West Point Military Academy. Because he had a year and a half of college, he did not think he would have to take the academic test given by West Point. He did, though,

65

and he failed. That failure only drove him more to be accepted by West Point. But he would have to wait another year to take the exam. He prepared well this time and passed. Davis was on his way to West Point.

TRYING TO REACH THE AIR

Although the silent treatment Davis received at West Point was hard on him, he did all he could to succeed. In October 1935 Davis applied to the United States Army Air Corps. He passed the physical exam and was on his way to becoming a member when he received a rejection letter. It explained that at the time there were no black units in the Air Corps. After all, there would be no way a black man could command white troops. Davis was devastated but still kept hope that in the future policies would be changed. He was in the Army, and he decided he would do the best job he could wherever he was sent.

While at West Point, Davis met a woman named Agatha Scott of New Haven, Connecticut. They married two weeks after Davis graduated from the academy, in 1936. She was the light of his life.

Davis was assigned to the 24th Infantry Regiment at Fort Benning, Georgia. Here, Davis and Agatha experienced more segregation. They were not allowed to join the officers' club. Their neighbors would not talk to them. Davis's own commander did not greet and introduce himself as tradition in the Army dictated.

GETTING HIS WINGS

In 1941 Davis and Agatha were sent to Fort Riley in Kansas. Here the treatment was lukewarm. Davis still could not join the all-white officers' club, and he and his wife had to use the movie theatre on base because it "allowed" blacks.

Suddenly, just a few weeks after his arrival, Davis was ordered to begin pilot training. He reasoned the turn-around decision saying, "It was obvious that the nation was going to be involved in the war in the immediate future, and no upsettingly radical social changes in the corps were to be permitted to interfere with its rapid mobilization."[3] The country would soon be at war with both Germany and Japan, and the military needed all the people and manpower it could find. The all-white Army Air Corps would create an all-black flying unit known as the 99th Fighter Squadron (originally named the 99th Pursuit Squadron).

Davis had to go through another physical in which the physician, having not heard about the new changes and creation of an all-black squadron, failed Davis. The physician said he had a medical disorder called epilepsy. Not to be

The P-40 Warhawk fighter was widely used at the beginning of World War II. Davis and the Tuskegee Airmen trained in and flew them in combat in North Africa, Italy, and Sicily.

deterred, Davis quickly got a second physical in which his epilepsy miraculously was "cured," and he passed. Davis was the first black commander of an all-black squadron. He trained for a year to become a pilot before being deployed. On March 7, 1942, Davis received his silver flying wings of the Army Air Force. He was officially a pilot.

THE TUSKEGEE AIRMEN

Finally, in 1943, Davis and twenty-three other pilots sailed across the Atlantic to join the war.[4] Known as the Tuskegee Airmen, they joined the 33rd Fighter Group in Tunisia, Africa, where they flew P-40 Warhawk aircraft. On June 2, 1943, Davis led his men on their first mission. They were to attack troops on Pantelleria Island, an enemy position between North Africa and Sicily. Davis remarked, "Combat flying was of course far more stressful than flying in a friendly area. . . . You had to work as a team with the other pilots in the formation and keep turning your head and eyes to areas of the sky where the enemy fighter was most likely to appear."[5]

The 99th Fighter Squadron then moved to Sicily, Italy, to continue the fight. The pilots performed well, delivering bombs on target. But the 99th soon came under attack, not by the enemy but by the U.S. Army. Some officers in the 33rd Fighter Group submitted letters stating that the

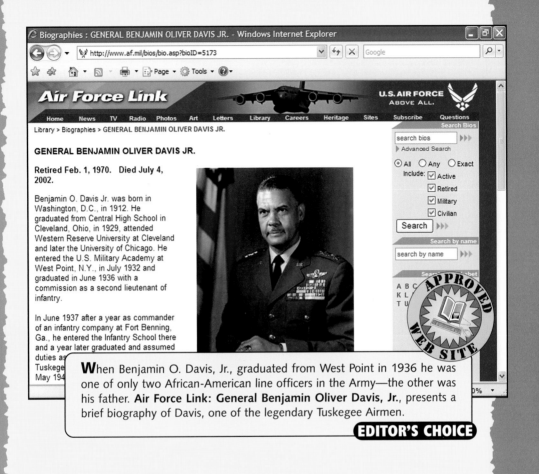

Biographies : GENERAL BENJAMIN OLIVER DAVIS JR. - Windows Internet Explorer

http://www.af.mil/bios/bio.asp?bioID=5173   Google

Page ▾   Tools ▾

Air Force Link   U.S. AIR FORCE
ABOVE ALL.

Home   News   TV   Radio   Photos   Art   Letters   Library   Careers   Heritage   Sites   Subscribe   Questions

Library > Biographies > GENERAL BENJAMIN OLIVER DAVIS JR.

GENERAL BENJAMIN OLIVER DAVIS JR.

Retired Feb. 1, 1970.   Died July 4, 2002.

Benjamin O. Davis Jr. was born in Washington, D.C., in 1912. He graduated from Central High School in Cleveland, Ohio, in 1929, attended Western Reserve University at Cleveland and later the University of Chicago. He entered the U.S. Military Academy at West Point, N.Y., in July 1932 and graduated in June 1936 with a commission as a second lieutenant of infantry.

In June 1937 after a year as commander of an infantry company at Fort Benning, Ga., he entered the Infantry School there and a year later graduated and assumed duties as Tuskege May 194

Search Bios
search bios
▶ Advanced Search
● All   ○ Any   ○ Exact
Include: ☑ Active
☑ Retired
☑ Military
☑ Civilian
Search ▶▶▶
Search by name
search by name   ▶▶▶

A B C
K L
T U

When Benjamin O. Davis, Jr., graduated from West Point in 1936 he was one of only two African-American line officers in the Army—the other was his father. **Air Force Link: General Benjamin Oliver Davis, Jr.**, presents a brief biography of Davis, one of the legendary Tuskegee Airmen.

EDITOR'S CHOICE

99th did not perform well at all. "The Negro type has not the proper reflexes to make a first-class fighter pilot," stated one letter.[6]

Davis was furious. He showed how the 99th had not only been successful in their missions but also flew six combat missions a day—more than white pilots. His arguments won and the 99th stayed in combat. Later, the Tuskegee Airmen would have a seven-to-one ratio of victories to losses.[7]

▲ Colonel Benjamin O. Davis (front left) listens to a briefing in Italy with his pilots. They proved the ability of African-American pilots, most notably by never losing a bomber to an enemy fighter during two hundred escort missions.

CHANGE ARRIVES

Davis was now commander of the 332nd Fighter Group. On March 24, 1945, he led his men on a sixteen hundred-mile round-trip escort mission to Berlin. Immediately, the Tuskegee Airmen were met head-on by the German enemy. The Tuskegee Airmen held their own, shooting down three M262 jets, which were new to the scene and very fast. They also damaged six other fighters. By contrast, none of the 332nd's bombers were destroyed, and only one of the Tuskegee Airmen was lost on the mission.

By the time the war ended, the Tuskegee Airmen had shot down 111 enemy aircraft and destroyed an additional 150 on the ground, far more in comparison to the 66 aircraft they lost to all causes in combat. They had crushed or disabled more than six hundred boxcars and other vehicles. They sank one destroyer and more than forty other boats and barges. And to top it off, not one of their bombers was lost to enemy fighters in two hundred escort missions to locations that were heavily defended.[8] Because of their achievement, the Air Force saw no reason to segregate blacks from whites. On July 26, 1948, President Harry S Truman issued an executive order to desegregate the United States military. The United States Air Force (USAF) became the first branch of military service to racially integrate.

General Davis was the first African American to hold the rank of general and retired wearing the three stars of a lieutenant general in 1970. President Bill Clinton awarded him his fourth star in 1998, making him a full general.

General Davis went on to serve at the USAF Headquarters in Washington, D.C. In 1953, as the Korean War was waged, he took command of the 51st Fighter-Interceptor Wing in Korea. He was soon promoted to brigadier general, becoming the first African American in the United States Air

Force to earn a star. He continued to serve his country until his retirement in 1970. He passed away on July 4, 2002.

When Davis joined the Army Air Force, he was the only black officer. Today, there are about four thousand.[9] Davis overcame racial segregation by proving that black men and women could handle the same kinds of jobs as white men and women. He wanted to fly and to serve his country and in doing so, he opened up doors for all people of color.

Neil Armstrong

Imagine being the first person to land on the moon. It would be both scary and exciting. Astronaut Neil Armstrong was the person who actually experienced this. As commander of the *Apollo 11* mission, he had to fly the lunar module *Eagle* safely to the moon. The National Aeronautics Space Administration (NASA) was in constant contact with Armstrong. "How does it look?" they radioed.

"The *Eagle* has wings," said Neil Armstrong.[1]

Flying with Neil Armstrong was Buzz Aldrin. The *Eagle* orbited the moon fourteen

Lifeline

1930: Born near Wapakoneta, Ohio, on August 5.

1949: Attends Purdue University on a Navy scholarship, but must leave for flight training.

1949–1952: Serves as a pilot in the U.S. Navy.

1952–1955: Finishes aeronautical engineering degree.

times before the astronauts could start to land. They slowly descended fifty thousand feet to the moon. The *Eagle* had a computer that was doing most of the work. Soon, it was time for Armstrong to take over the controls and land the lunar module himself.

The area chosen was called the Sea of Tranquility. It was a good area, clear of boulders and perfect for a landing. But things did not go as planned. The computer used to land the *Eagle* was leading the spaceship to an area the size of a football field filled with boulders. This would be okay as long as Armstrong did not hit a big boulder and cause structural damage. After all, they had to launch back into space in the same lunar module.

The *Eagle* was almost out of fuel. With a steady hand, Armstrong controlled the *Eagle* landing. It dropped about twenty feet per

1956–1962: Becomes a test pilot.

1966: Command pilot on the Gemini 8 space mission.

1970: Resigns from astronaut corps.

1956: Marries Janet Shearon.

1962: Transfers to NASA's astronaut corps.

1969: Commands the Apollo 11 mission. Becomes the first person to walk on the moon on July 20.

second. Armstrong slowed the *Eagle* to nine feet per second. Among the boulders, he found a smooth area to land. Thrusters were ignited and a plume of dust rose. Probes that dangled from the *Eagle* touched the moon first. Then, the *Eagle* settled down gently.

"Houston, Tranquility base here. The *Eagle* has landed."[2] Armstrong sounded calm. The moon landing had gone well. It was July 20, 1969, at 4:17 in the afternoon, Eastern Daylight Time.

ACTIVE YOUTH

Neil Armstrong was born on his grandparents' farm near Wapakoneta, Ohio. He was born on August 5, 1930, to Stephen and Viola Armstrong.

Apollo 11 Lunar Surface Journal

This NASA Web site contains a complete archive of the *Apollo 11* mission, including images, audio, and video.

Access this Web site from http://www.myreportlinks.com

Armstrong had a brother, Dean, and sister, June. His father was an auditor for the state of Ohio.

When Armstrong was two years old, his father took him to Cleveland Airport to see the 1932 National Air Races. Four years later, Armstrong's father took him for his first airplane ride. The airplane was a Ford Trimotor nicknamed the "Old Tin Goose." His father said later, "Those old Ford Trimotors; they really rattled. I was scared to death and Neil enjoyed it."[3]

As a child, Armstrong had a strange recurring dream. "I could, by holding my breath, hover over the ground. Nothing much happened. I neither flew nor fell in those dreams; I just hovered."[4] Armstrong was never sure what his dream meant. Looking back, many saw it as a sign of things to come.

TAKING OFF

"I began to focus on aviation probably at age eight or nine," Armstrong recalls.[5] He became interested in building model airplanes. He chose balsa wood and tissue paper to make most of his planes. The idea of adding an engine to his models seemed extravagant since "motors cost extra money and required gasoline—both of which were in short supply during World War II."[6] Instead, he used rubber bands to propel his models. He hung models from his bedroom ceiling and sometimes sent them sailing out his bedroom window.

Armstrong loved building the model airplanes more than actually flying them. He thought he wanted to be an aircraft designer. He read a lot of aviation magazines like *Flight and Air Trails* and *Model Airplane News*.

In his teens, Armstrong worked at a drugstore. Instead of buying models with his earnings, he saved for flying lessons. Armstrong would ride his bike to Wapakoneta Airfield, which had old army planes and trainers. Here, he learned to fly and by the age of sixteen, he had his student pilot's license. It was the summer of 1946. A few weeks later, he flew his first solo.

Armstrong was an active young boy, though shy. He did very well in school and graduated from Blume High School in 1947, eleventh in his class. His mother encouraged Neil to go to college.

COMBAT IN KOREA

Armstrong wanted to earn a degree in aeronautical engineering. He would need financial aid to help pay for college, so he applied for a United States Navy scholarship. He was accepted and was allowed to pick the college of his choice. Armstrong attended classes at Purdue University in West Lafayette, Indiana. But after a year and a half, the Navy ordered him to Pensacola, Florida, for flight training.

In June 1950 the Korean War began. Two months later, Armstrong received his Navy "wings of gold." He was now a pilot. Armstrong joined VF-51 in San Diego, California. On January 5, 1951, Armstrong flew his first flight in a Grumman F9F-2B Panther. He became the youngest man in his unit to fly combat missions in Korea.

Armstrong trained as a naval pilot to fight air-to-air combat, but when no enemy planes were in the area, his mission changed to a fighter-bomber. Instead of shooting down MiGs (Soviet military fighter aircraft), he dropped bombs on targets such as bridges and tunnels.

While on assignment once, Armstrong almost went down when the wing of his plane clipped a cable that was strung at five hundred feet across a valley in North Korea. The cable had been set as a booby trap. Part of the wing tore loose, and his plane spun out of control, but Armstrong was able to recover and fly back to the aircraft carrier.

A military aviation historian has noted that "Armstrong displayed in this combat experience the qualities of courage and skill that would lead to his selection as the commander of the first lunar landing mission in 1969."[7] By the end of the Korean War, Armstrong had flown seventy-eight combat missions. He was awarded three air medals.

81

🧪 THE ROCKET PLANE

In 1952 Armstrong returned to Purdue University. He received his bachelor's degree in aeronautical engineering. He also met his wife, Janet Shearon. They were married in 1956. Two sons, Eric and

Mark, and a daughter, Karen followed. Sadly, Karen died of a brain tumor before she was three years old.

Armstrong had two career options: He could return to the Navy or find work elsewhere. He chose to become a research pilot. In 1955 he worked at Lewis Flight Propulsion Lab in Cleveland, Ohio. Then, from 1956 to 1962, Armstrong was a test pilot for NASA's Flight Research Center. He and his family moved to Edwards Air Force Base in California.

As a NASA test pilot, Armstrong piloted or served as copilot in every research plane flown at Edwards Air Force Base. This included the X-15 rocket plane. He was one of the first pilots to fly a rocket plane. It had two rocket engines, and flew at 4,520 miles per hour (over five times the speed of sound) and as high as 354,000 feet. From this high up, Earth looked like an orb.

Armstrong has flown over two hundred different kinds of aircraft including the rocket-powered X-15.

83

In the early 1960s, the United States was eager to conquer outer space. The space race was on, with Russia as a fierce competitor. At this time, Russia was far ahead of the United States in space technology. John F. Kennedy, president of the United States from 1961 to 1963, had a dream to put a person on the moon. The space program in the United States grew, and Armstrong was a big part of it.

MERCURY AND GEMINI

NASA first established the Mercury program. This put people in space for the first time. All missions were successful. Next came the Gemini program. *Gemini 8* was the eighth mission in the Gemini series. Armstrong was the command pilot and David Scott was the copilot. The flight lasted about ten hours.

There were two objectives these astronauts wanted to accomplish: docking with another target vehicle and spending time outside the vehicle in outer space. The successful docking, which was executed by Armstrong, was the first of its kind. *Gemini 8* docked with a spacecraft called *Agena*. *Agena* was part of a rocket. It had been launched and put into orbit about the same time as *Gemini 8*. However, the planned space walk, which would have been done by Scott, had to be canceled.

Shortly after docking, a thruster became jammed and caused the *Gemini 8* to spin. The only way to stop from spinning was to detach from *Agena* and head back to Earth. As Armstrong and Scott tried to regain control, they lost radio contact with NASA. Finally, Armstrong regained control and radioed to NASA that the craft had been steadied. They landed as planned in the ocean. Still feeling sick from the spinning, they waited to be rescued.

Armstrong's ability to remain calm and regain control of a spacecraft gone wild were major factors in his being chosen for the *Apollo 11* mission—the journey to the moon. On January 9, 1969, three men were selected for this adventure: Neil Armstrong, Buzz Aldrin, and Michael Collins. By May, they had spent many hours training in simulators. They were ready to actually try reaching the moon.

FIRST MAN ON THE MOON

On July 16, 1969, Armstrong, Aldrin, and Collins put on their bulky space suits and headed to the launchpad. Excitement filled the air as millions of people around the world prepared to watch this great event. Man had flown in outer space, but had not walked on the moon. *Apollo 11* lifted off without any problems and the men were on their way.

Being the
First Man
on the Moon

Neil Armstrong stepped into history when he became the first person to set foot on the moon, but since then, he has remained a very private person. This *60 Minutes* interview offers insights into perhaps the most famous person we know so little about.

Access this Web site from http://www.myreportlinks.com

It would be a four-day journey for the men, but with plenty to do. When they reached the moon's orbit, they would fly the *Eagle* down to the surface of the moon. The command module, *Columbia*, piloted by Collins, would circle the moon twelve times. Then the *Eagle*, with Armstrong and Aldrin aboard, would depart from the *Columbia* and land on the thirteenth orbit. Armstrong would pilot the *Eagle*.

At 10:56 P.M. Eastern Daylight Time on July 20, 1969, Armstrong stepped onto the moon with his left foot. He spoke the now famous words, "That's one small step for man, one giant leap for mankind."[8]

▲ *The* Saturn V *rocket lifts off on July 16, 1969, launching the* Apollo 11 *astronauts into space.*

"The surface is fine and powdery, it adheres in fine layers, like powered charcoal, to the soles and side of my foot," he said. "I can see footprints of my boots and the treads in the fine sandy particles."[9]

Buzz Aldrin joined him on the moon. For two hours they gathered samples, planted an American flag, and took photos. They also left a bronze plaque that read:

HERE MEN FROM THE PLANET EARTH

FIRST SET FOOT UPON THE MOON

JULY 1969 A.D.

WE CAME IN PEACE FOR ALL MANKIND.[10]

Soon it was time to return. Armstrong and Aldrin rejoined the *Columbia*, which had been orbiting the moon. They returned to Earth four days later and landed in the Pacific Ocean. A helicopter picked them up and brought them safely to the USS *Hornet*, an aircraft carrier. The men were greeted with tremendous fanfare. The first men to walk on the moon were heroes to most Americans. President John F. Kennedy's dream had come true.

SETTING THE LIMIT

Armstrong resigned from the astronaut corps in 1970. Just as shy and quiet as he was in his youth, he did not like attention from the public. He went on to teach aeronautical engineering and work on

On July 20, 1969, the human race accomplished its single greatest technological achievement of all time when a human first set foot on another celestial body.

Six hours after landing at 4:17 p.m. Eastern Daylight Time (with less than 30 seconds of fuel remaining), Neil A. Armstrong took the "Small Step" into our greater future when he stepped off the Lunar Module, named "Eagle," onto the surface of the Moon, from which he could look up and see Earth in the heavens as no one had done before him.

Apollo 11 Thirtieth Anniversary

The *Apollo 11* **Thirtieth Anniversary** site from NASA includes biographies of the *Apollo 11* astronauts, images of Neil Armstrong's historic first steps on the moon, a time line, and lots of other primary-source information.

EDITOR'S CHOICE

Access this Web site from http://www.myreportlinks.com

research and development, much preferring the quiet life outside the public eye.

Flight took on a whole new meaning when humanity traveled to outer space. No longer were people confined to Earth's blue skies; they could travel beyond. Armstrong pushed the limits of not only what humankind could do, but also of what machines could do. Today, the United States has a growing space program because of Armstrong and other enthusiastic aviators like Sally Ride, the first woman in space.

Sally Ride

Flying in outer space used to be a career only open to men. Sally Ride changed that. She became the first woman to orbit the earth. While growing up in the late 1950s and 1960s, she felt that there was a fixed view that girls should not strive for jobs dominated by men. Getting into the newly developed space program was difficult, especially for women. The year Ride applied, eight thousand men and women also applied for the program. Of the thirty-five people selected,

Lifeline

1951: Born in Los Angeles, California, on May 26.

1973: Receives bachelor's degrees in physics and English from Stanford University.

1975: Receives master's degree in physics from Stanford.

1977: Applies to become an astronaut.

six were women. Sally Ride was one of them.

⚗ GROWING UP

Sally Kristen Ride was born in Los Angeles, California, on May 26, 1951. She is the oldest daughter of two born to Dale and Joyce Ride. Ride was a natural-born athlete. As a child, she liked to play baseball and football with the neighborhood boys. She dreamed about playing baseball with her favorite team, the Los Angeles Dodgers. She had other dreams, too, like flying in outer space.

Ride remembered how much the new space program impacted her life even at a young age. "I remember the early days of the space program. In elementary school, our teacher rolled in a TV set and we watched some of the first space missions. It really ignited my interest."[1] Little did she know that her childhood dream would come true.

Chapter 7

1978: Chosen as an astronaut candidate; receives Ph.D. degree in physics from Stanford.

1983: First shuttle mission on June 18, becoming the first woman in space.

1984: Second shuttle mission.

1986: Serves on commission investigating the Challenger tragedy.

1987: Retires from NASA.

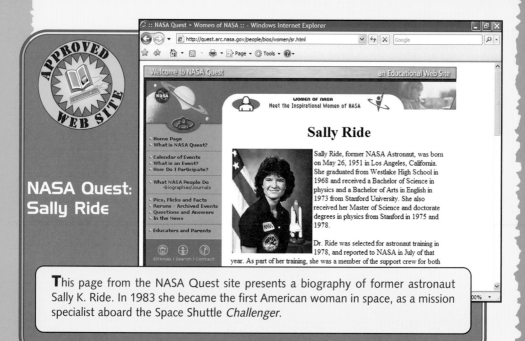

NASA Quest: Sally Ride

Sally Ride

Sally Ride, former NASA Astronaut, was born on May 26, 1951 in Los Angeles, California. She graduated from Westlake High School in 1968 and received a Bachelor of Science in physics and a Bachelor of Arts in English in 1973 from Stanford University. She also received her Master of Science and doctorate degrees in physics from Stanford in 1975 and 1978.

Dr. Ride was selected for astronaut training in 1978, and reported to NASA in July of that year. As part of her training, she was a member of the support crew for both

This page from the NASA Quest site presents a biography of former astronaut Sally K. Ride. In 1983 she became the first American woman in space, as a mission specialist aboard the Space Shuttle *Challenger*.

Access this Web site from http://www.myreportlinks.com

When Ride was nine years old, her father quit his job, sold the house, and moved the family to Europe. While touring Spain, she learned about tennis. Ride studied with Alice Marble, a Wimbledon champion, and soon excelled at the sport. She placed eighteenth in the junior tennis circuit competition. Tennis was good for young Sally Ride. It taught her discipline and self-control.

🧪 MATH AND SCIENCE RULE

When the Ride family returned to the United States a year later, Sally attended Portola Junior High. She liked math and science and did well. She continued to play tennis and received a tennis scholarship to Westlake High School, an all-girls private school, in Beverly Hills, California. Here, she focused her studies on the sciences like chemistry and physics. She also studied math, such as calculus and trigonometry. Ride seriously considered becoming a professional tennis player, but decided to give college a try.

Ride applied and was accepted to Swarthmore College in Pennsylvania. However, she was not happy there. After a year and a half, she quit. "I decided, 'What was I thinking? I should have been a professional tennis player,' and I quit college, . . . moved back to Southern California, and actually focused on tennis for about three months before I saw the light and transferred to Stanford, went back to school."[2]

WANTED: ASTRONAUTS

At Stanford, Ride could get her education and still play tennis. She majored in physics, but at times found this to be overwhelming. To balance all the math and science classes, Ride took English. She found she loved it. When she graduated in 1973, she had her bachelor of science degree in physics and her bachelor of arts degree in English.

Ride continued her education by entering Stanford University's master's program in astrophysics. Ride studied the physical and chemical characteristics of celestial matter, focusing on rays given off by stars.

Just as Ride was finishing her doctorate degree in 1977, she happened to browse through a newspaper and saw an ad. It was placed by NASA. They were looking for astronauts. ". . . [T]he moment I saw that, I knew that that's what I wanted to do. Not that I wanted to leave physics, I loved it, but I wanted to apply to the astronaut corps and see whether NASA would take me, and see whether I could have the opportunity to go on that adventure."[3]

NASA was specifically looking for young scientists to become mission specialists. The astronaut corps consisted of many test pilots and aviators. NASA wanted scientists who would work on the space shuttle conducting experiments. The space shuttle program was relatively new.

The Call

Ride applied for the position but did not expect to be chosen. Then a call arrived to her on January 16, 1978, saying that she was one of thirty-five people accepted to the space shuttle program. Because of her research on free-electron lasers, NASA hoped her work could be used to develop a method of sending energy from a space station back to Earth. Ride was beyond excited. Then the reality hit her as she recalled thinking, "Oh my

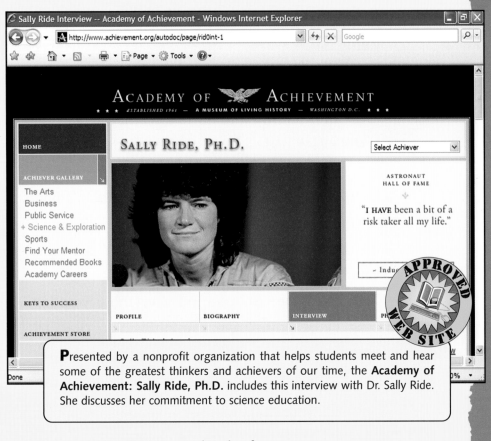

http://www.achievement.org/autodoc/page/rid0int-1

ACADEMY OF ACHIEVEMENT
★ ★ ★ *ESTABLISHED 1961* — A MUSEUM OF LIVING HISTORY — *WASHINGTON D.C.* ★ ★ ★

SALLY RIDE, PH.D.

HOME

ACHIEVER GALLERY
The Arts
Business
Public Service
+ Science & Exploration
Sports
Find Your Mentor
Recommended Books
Academy Careers

KEYS TO SUCCESS

ACHIEVEMENT STORE

Select Achiever

ASTRONAUT
HALL OF FAME

"I HAVE been a bit of a
risk taker all my life."

PROFILE   BIOGRAPHY   INTERVIEW

APPROVED WEB SITE

Presented by a nonprofit organization that helps students meet and hear some of the greatest thinkers and achievers of our time, the **Academy of Achievement: Sally Ride, Ph.D.** includes this interview with Dr. Sally Ride. She discusses her commitment to science education.

gosh, I am going to be the first woman to get to go up, representing this country."[4] Ride finished her studies at Stanford with a doctorate in physics, and reported to the Lyndon Johnson Space Center in Houston, Texas. There she met astronomer Steve Hawley, who was also accepted to the program. He and Ride married in 1982, but would divorce five years later.

ASTRONAUT TRAINING

The training was intense, as it is for all astronauts. In one such exercise, Ride was dropped from an airplane over cold water. Wearing a space suit and strapped into an open parachute, she had to free herself while being dragged in the water. This training would prepare her for if she landed in water after reentry into Earth's orbit.

Ride also had to learn to deal with nausea, a common problem for astronauts. She was one of the few who did not get sick. The physical training was not as hard as Ride expected. But the mental training was difficult. Ride described it this way: "You have to learn everything there is to know about the Space Shuttle and everything you are going to be doing, and everything you need to know if something goes wrong, and then once you have learned it all, you have to practice, practice, practice, practice, practice, practice, practice until everything is second nature, so it's a very, very difficult training, and it takes years."[5]

SHOOTING FOR THE STARS

Stepping onto the launchpad at Kennedy Space Center in Florida and looking at a thirty-story-high space shuttle is daunting for any person, even a well-trained astronaut. It was June 18, 1983, when Sally Ride, mission specialist, would be the first American woman to launch into space. *Challenger* was the name of the space shuttle, commanded by Robert Crippen.

Sally Ride, wearing a communications headset, floats next to the *Challenger*'s mid-deck airlock hatch.

This was to be the seventh space shuttle flight carried out by the NASA space program. At that time, it was the biggest crew to blast off—four men and one woman. The shuttle carried two communications satellites that would come back to Earth. Two other satellites would be put in Earth's orbit. This shuttle mission also took into space twenty experiments created by high school students.

RIDE IN SPACE

The first day, two satellites for Indonesia and Canada were launched. Ride launched ANIK-C, a Canadian communications satellite. This would help route television, TELEX, and telephone signals throughout North America. The second satellite, Palapa B, was launched to provide a million people with telephone service in Indonesia.

Ride also worked a robotic arm. Its claw-like hand was used to reach out and grab a satellite. She used the arm to bring the satellite back to the shuttle's cargo bay and then release it. This was the first time a robotic arm was used in outer space. Ride and the crew experimented with the robotic arm for nine hours.

Seven separate experiments were also conducted. These experiments were called Getaway Special (GAS) experiments. They included observation of crystal growth, and a study of movement

Challenger orbits Earth during Sally Ride's first mission in space. It was the second vehicle in NASA's space shuttle fleet.

and seedling growth. The astronauts on this mission were busy. Ride's first view of Earth from outer space was awe-inspiring. She said:

> The view of Earth is absolutely spectacular, and the feeling of looking back and seeing your planet as a planet is just an amazing feeling. . . . [I]t makes you appreciate, actually, how fragile our existence is. You can look at Earth's horizon and see this really, really thin royal blue line right along the horizon, . . . and it's about as thick as the fuzz on a tennis ball, and it's everything that separates us from the vacuum of space. If we didn't have that atmosphere, we wouldn't be here, and if we do anything to destroy that atmosphere, we won't be here.[6]

The shuttle landed safely six days later on June 24 at Edwards Air Force Base in California. *Challenger* had orbited Earth ninety-seven times and traveled over 2 million miles.

Ride took her second flight in space on October 5, 1984. This was the thirteenth shuttle mission on *Challenger* and like before, it was commanded by Robert Crippen. During their eight-day mission, the crew deployed the Earth Radiation Budget Satellite. They also conducted scientific observations of Earth, and demonstrated the potential for satellite refueling by astronauts. The mission lasted 197 hours, and concluded with a landing at the Kennedy Space Center in Florida.[7]

CHALLENGER DISASTER

As Sally Ride prepared for her third shuttle mission, tragedy struck *Challenger* and the space shuttle program. On January 28, 1986, *Challenger* exploded in what looked like a display of fireworks, about seventy-three seconds after liftoff. Everyone on board was killed, including two civilians. Ride was deeply affected by the loss not only because she had flown on *Challenger* before, but also because four of the astronauts were from her original class of thirty-five. She knew them very well.

Ride was appointed to a twelve-member commission to figure out what had gone wrong with the shuttle. They learned that the explosion was caused by the failure of rubber seals called O-rings. The space shuttle program was put on hold and so was Ride's career as an astronaut. This did not matter. She realized on her second space shuttle flight that she really did love physics and science and decided now was a good time to get back into it.

WRITING AND PHYSICS

In 1986 Ride wrote and published a book called *To Space and Back* and dedicated it to the crew lost in the *Challenger* explosion. She received many honors including induction into the National Women's

35 Who Made a Difference: Sally Ride | Science & Nature | Smithsonian Magazine - Windows Internet Explorer

http://www.smithsonianmag.com/science-nature/10013151.html

Smithsonian.com

ARCHIVE   SHOP   MEMBER SERVICES   EMAI

Air & Space magazine | goSmithsonian | Smithsoni

| Home | History & Archaeology | People & Places | Science & Nature | Arts & Culture | Travel | Photos & Videos | Subscribe |

Anthropology & Behavior   Dinosaurs   Environment   Technology & Space   Wildlife

SCIENCE & NATURE

35 Who Made a Difference: Sally Ride

A generation later, the first female astronaut is still on a mission

By K.C. Cole
Smithso...   November 2005

Dr. Sally Ride discusses the importance of encouraging young girls to pursue the sciences on the *Smithsonian* Magazine: **35 Who Made a Difference—Sally Ride** Web site.

Hall of Fame. Ride officially left the astronaut's corps in May 1987.

Ride continues her research in physics. She tours the country talking to students about the sciences, becoming an astronaut, and pursuing dreams. She has published several books for children. Ride knows from her own experience that dreams can come true with a good education and hard work. She especially encourages young girls to get involved in science, and she has started the Sally Ride Academy for educators, as well as the

Sally Ride Science Festival for girls in grades five through eight.

Ride stated, "Science is an exciting field for everyone. Whether it's as an astronaut or an engineer in mission control or a scientist receiving data from Mars, there are lots of exciting possibilities and all are open to women as well as to men. The most important thing is to get a good background in science while you're in school."[8]

Eileen Collins

When Eileen Collins was at summer camp at Harris Hill in Elmira, New York, she gazed up at the gliders. She knew then that she wanted to fly. At the announcement of her first space mission, she recalled: "When I was a child, I dreamed about space— I admired pilots, astronauts, and I've admired explorers of all kinds. It was only a dream that I would someday be one of them.

Lifeline

1975: Begins flying lessons at a local airport.

1978: Receives a bachelor of arts degree in mathematics and economics

1986: Gets master's of science degree in operations research.

1956: Born in Elmira, New York, on November 19.

1976: Receives associates degree in mathematics and science.

1979: Graduates from Air Force Undergraduate Pilot Training.

It is my hope that all children, boys and girls, will see this mission and be inspired to reach for their dreams, because dreams do come true!"[1]

🜃 GROWING UP

Collins was born in Elmira, New York, on November 19, 1956. She has two brothers and a sister. Her parents are Jim and Rose Collins. Collins's father was a surveyor and postal worker.

Aviation surrounded Collins from a young age. Her hometown, Elmira, is called the "soaring capital of America" for its rich history in aviation and collection of period planes. Even though Collins's parents did not have the money to spend on flying lessons, they would take Collins to the nearby Elmira-Corning Regional Airport or Harris Hill's glider field to watch planes and gliders take off and land.

1990: Selected by NASA.

1995: First space shuttle mission begins, becoming first woman shuttle pilot on February 3.

1999: Third shuttle mission, becoming the first woman shuttle commander on July 23.

2006: Retires from NASA.

1989: Applies to NASA's astronaut program; earns master of arts degree in space systems management.

1991: Becomes an astronaut.

1997: Second shuttle mission.

2005: Fourth shuttle mission; retires from Air Force.

Pages in the History of Elmira | Eileen Collins: Elmira's Space Hero - Windows Internet Explorer

http://www.cityofelmira.net/history/eileen_collins.html

Page ▾ Tools ▾

PAGES IN THE HISTORY OF ELMIRA

Honoring the Past, Building the Future

Chemung County
New York

Eileen Collins: Elmira's Space Hero

Pages in History Index
Brian Williams
Civil War Prison Camp
Crystal Eastman
Eileen Collins
Ernie Davis
Flood of 1972
Hal Roach
John W. Jones
Mark Twain
Postcards in History
Soaring
Tho...
Un...

Ba...

Conta...
Press Ro...
Communi...
Elmira Ma...

"When I was a child, I dreamed about space - I admired pilots, astronauts, and I've admired explorers of all kinds. It was only a dream that I would someday be one of them. It is my hope that all children, boys and girls, will see this mission and be inspired to reach for their dreams, because dreams do come true!" - Eileen Collins, astronaut

Colonel Eileen Marie Collins made history when she became the first woman to command a space shuttle mission, STS-93 *Columbia*, on July 22-27, 1999. A long and successful road led Collins to that historical

Historical Resources
Chemung County Historical Society
415 E. Water Street
Elmira, NY 14901
(607) 734-4167
»website

Steele Memorial Library
101 E. Church Street
Elmira, NY 14901
(607) 733-9176
»website

Center for Mark Twain Studies at Elmira College
One Park Place
Elmira, NY 14901
(607) 735-1941
»website

John Jones Museum

Done

Astronaut Eileen Collins was born in Elmira, New York, in 1956, and grew up there, where her love of space began with her fondness for *Star Trek*. Read **Eileen Collins: Elmira's Space Hero** to learn more about the childhood and career of one of this city's most famous daughters.

As a young girl, Collins read books about the Wright brothers, and one of her heroes was Amelia Earhart. But she really loved to watch a television program called *Star Trek*. "Eileen's love of flying really started with *Star Trek*," said her mother, Rose. "She used to come straight home from school and watch it whenever she could."[2]

🧪 CAN I FLY NOW?

Collins attended local schools in Elmira and did well. Her favorite subjects were math and science.

In high school, she enjoyed taking language. But when she entered college, she decided to major in math because that was where her strength was. "I try to encourage young people to take a variety of courses in school and find out what you really like, because usually what you like is what you're going to do well at."[3]

Collins wanted to learn to fly so badly that she started working at a pizza place to save up the money for lessons when she was sixteen. It took her three years to save one thousand dollars, but she did it. She went to the local airport and said, "Teach me how to fly!" Collins started her training in a Cessna aircraft and eventually got her pilot's license.

STUDENT PILOT

Money was still tight for her family, so Collins went to Corning Community College for two years. She received her associate's degree in mathematics and science in 1976. Then she went on to Syracuse University where she received her bachelor's degree in mathematics and economics. While at Syracuse, Collins joined the Air Force Reserve Officer Training Corps and entered the Air Force Undergraduate Pilot Training Program in 1978.

Collins was one of the first women to go straight from college into the pilot training

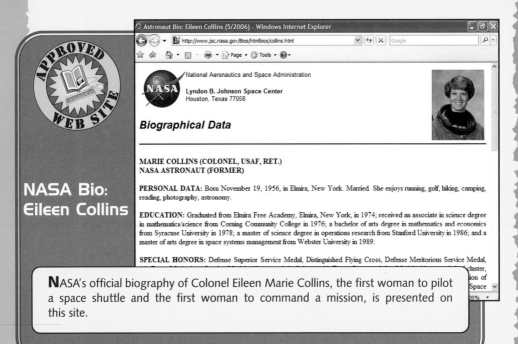

NASA Bio:
Eileen Collins

NASA's official biography of Colonel Eileen Marie Collins, the first woman to pilot a space shuttle and the first woman to command a mission, is presented on this site.

Access this Web site from http://www.myreportlinks.com

program. She felt that this was the biggest break she ever got in her life. It led Collins to pursuing her second dream—becoming an astronaut. The year she entered the Air Force just happened to be the same year that NASA opened the shuttle program to women. While she was training to be a pilot, the shuttle class of 1978 visited the young pilots. Ater that, Collins knew she wanted to be an astronaut.

Collins spent several years in the Air Force. She flew T-38s as an instructor pilot and the C-141 cargo jet as aircraft commander. Collins received her master's degree in operations research from Stanford University, as well as her master's degree in space systems management from Webster University. During this time, Collins met her husband, Pat Youngs. He also flew C-141s in the Air Force. They married in 1987 and had two children.

DREAMS DO COME TRUE

The space shuttle program had been rocked to its core when the shuttle *Challenger* exploded on January 28, 1986. Many people did not think the program would continue. It did and brought in many new people wishing to fly to outer space. Collins was one of them.

In 1989 Collins applied to the astronaut program. Her degrees as well as her pilot training in the Air Force allowed her to apply to both the pilot and mission specialist positions. NASA accepted Collins to be a pilot in 1990. The following year, in July, Collins qualified as an astronaut and shuttle pilot.

Finally, on February 3, 1995, Collins flew to space. She was the first woman to pilot a space shuttle. The mission was called STS-63, and it was a joint undertaking between Russia and the United States. Collins was the pilot aboard the Space Shuttle *Discovery*. While in space, the astronauts on *Discovery* rendezvoused and flew around the Russian space station, *Mir*. The mission was important and a first of its kind. Even though

The Space Shuttle *Discovery* is rolled out to the landing pad for Collins's first mission as shuttle commander.

Discovery did not dock at *Mir*, the Americans on board were the first to see the Russian space station. The mission also prepared for future dockings. That same year, Collins was awarded a place in the National Women's Hall of Fame in Seneca, New York.[4]

On Collins's second flight, from May 15 to 24, 1997, she piloted *Atlantis* to dock with *Mir*. It was the sixth time Americans had docked with *Mir*, but Collins's first. They delivered supplies, conducted experiments, and saw how a space station worked.

The third mission to outer space, called STS-93, was in the *Columbia*. It launched on July 23,

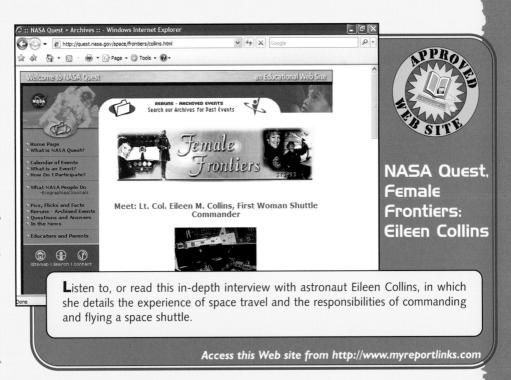

NASA Quest, Female Frontiers: Eileen Collins

Listen to, or read this in-depth interview with astronaut Eileen Collins, in which she details the experience of space travel and the responsibilities of commanding and flying a space shuttle.

Access this Web site from http://www.myreportlinks.com

1999, at 12:31 A.M. Eastern Daylight Time. It lasted four days, twenty-two hours, and fifty minutes. Again, Collins made history. She became the first woman to command a space shuttle mission. This time, the team of astronauts deployed the Chandra X-ray Observatory. The observatory contains telescopes that allow scientists to study phenomena such as exploding stars, quasars, and black holes.

On February 2, 2003, as the Space Shuttle *Columbia* was reentering Earth's atmosphere, it exploded, killing everyone on board. Again, the space shuttle program was put on hold and so was Collins's dream to fly in space. Despite the setback, Collins and her crew continued to work on a fourth mission. When the space shuttle program was up and running again, Collins was ready to fly in space.

ALWAYS AN EXPLORER

Collins was commander of the first space shuttle flight after the *Columbia* disaster. The mission was called NASA's Return to Flight on the Space Shuttle *Discovery*. It launched on July 26, 2005. This mission was important. It was the first flight since the *Columbia* disaster and studies were being conducted on ways to keep the crew and spacecraft safe. They were also delivering supplies to the International Space Station. Collins

Mission Commander Collins gets ready for the first space shuttle mission after the *Columbia* tragedy. The orange suit she is wearing protects astronauts against cold temperatures and loss of air pressure.

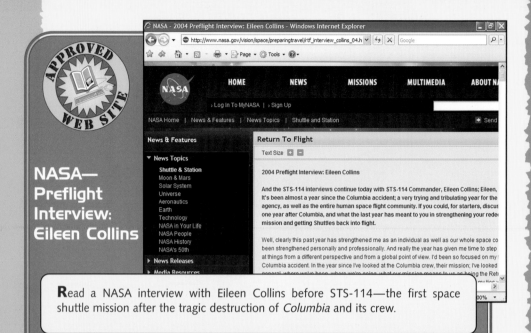

NASA—
Preflight
Interview:
Eileen Collins

NASA - 2004 Preflight Interview: Eileen Collins - Windows Internet Explorer

http://www.nasa.gov/vision/space/preparingtravel/rtf_interview_collins_04.h

Google

HOME   NEWS   MISSIONS   MULTIMEDIA   ABOUT N

› Log In To MyNASA   › Sign Up

NASA Home | News & Features | News Topics | Shuttle and Station   ➡ Send

News & Features

▼ News Topics

Shuttle & Station
Moon & Mars
Solar System
Universe
Aeronautics
Earth
Technology
NASA in Your Life
NASA People
NASA History
NASA's 50th

▶ News Releases
▶ Media Resources

Return To Flight

Text Size ➕ ➖

2004 Preflight Interview: Eileen Collins

And the STS-114 interviews continue today with STS-114 Commander, Eileen Collins; Eileen, it's been almost a year since the Columbia accident; a very trying and tribulating year for the agency, as well as the entire human space flight community. If you could, for starters, discuss one year after Columbia, and what the last year has meant to you in strengthening your rede mission and getting Shuttles back into flight.

Well, clearly this past year has strengthened me as an individual as well as our whole space co been strengthened personally and professionally. And really the year has given me time to step at things from a different perspective and from a global point of view. I'd been so focused on my Columbia accident. In the year since I've looked at the Columbia crew, their mission; I've looked

Read a NASA interview with Eileen Collins before STS-114—the first space shuttle mission after the tragic destruction of *Columbia* and its crew.

Access this Web site from http://www.myreportlinks.com

was very confident. "We're a nation of explorers. We are the kind of people who want to go out and learn new things, and I would say take risks, but take calculated risks that are studied and understood."[5]

In 2005 Collins retired from the Air Force. Later, on May 1, 2006, Eileen Collins retired from NASA. She wanted to spend more time with her family and pursue other interests. Also, as Collins explained, "We have many astronauts in this office who haven't even flown one flight. It's time for me to step aside and give the young guys a chance to fly."[6] However, she decided to continue with a non-NASA job in the aerospace industry. She hopes to continue to encourage and educate young people to pursue careers in the industry.

Collins says, "I find as a woman, maybe I can encourage other women to go into this field. I think that is really an opportunity that I have that I take seriously."[7]

Report Links

The Internet sites described below can be accessed at
http://www.myreportlinks.com

▶**The Wright Brothers: The Invention of the Aerial Age**
Editor's Choice A Smithsonian site profiles the Wright brothers, their historic flight, and aviation history.

▶**Amelia Earhart Birthplace Museum**
Editor's Choice Take an online tour of Amelia Earhart's birthplace, now a museum.

▶**The American Experience—Lindbergh**
Editor's Choice PBS examines the life of Charles A. Lindbergh, the first to fly solo across the Atlantic.

▶**Air Force Link: General Benjamin Oliver Davis, Jr.**
^^Editor's Choice^^ Read the United States Air Force's brief biography of General Benjamin O. Davis, Jr.

▶**Women in Aviation and Space History**
Editor's Choice Learn more about women who have become pioneers and leaders in aviation and space.

▶*Apollo 11* **Thirtieth Anniversary**
Editor's Choice NASA commemorates the thirtieth anniversary of the *Apollo 11* moon landing.

▶**Academy of Achievement: Sally Ride, Ph.D.**
An interview with former astronaut Sally Ride is featured.

▶**The American Experience—Fly Girls: Bessie Coleman**
PBS presents a brief biography of Bessie Coleman, the first African American to receive a pilot's license.

▶**Amelia Earhart**
Learn more about the brief but courageous life of aviation pioneer Amelia Earhart.

▶*Apollo 11* **Lunar Surface Journal**
Explore NASA's archive of the *Apollo 11* mission.

▶**Being the First Man on the Moon**
Watch or read an interview with Neil Armstrong from the CBS news program *60 Minutes*.

▶**Benjamin O. Davis, Jr. Collection**
Read about the life of Benjamin O. Davis, Jr., from the National Air and Space Museum's archives.

▶**Bessie Coleman**
The achievements of aviation pioneer Bessie Coleman are highlighted on this government site.

▶**Black Wings: African-American Pioneer Aviators**
This Smithsonian site chronicles the struggles and triumphs of pioneering African-American pilots.

▶**Charles Augustus Lindbergh**
Learn more about the life and achievements of Charles A. Lindbergh from this government site.

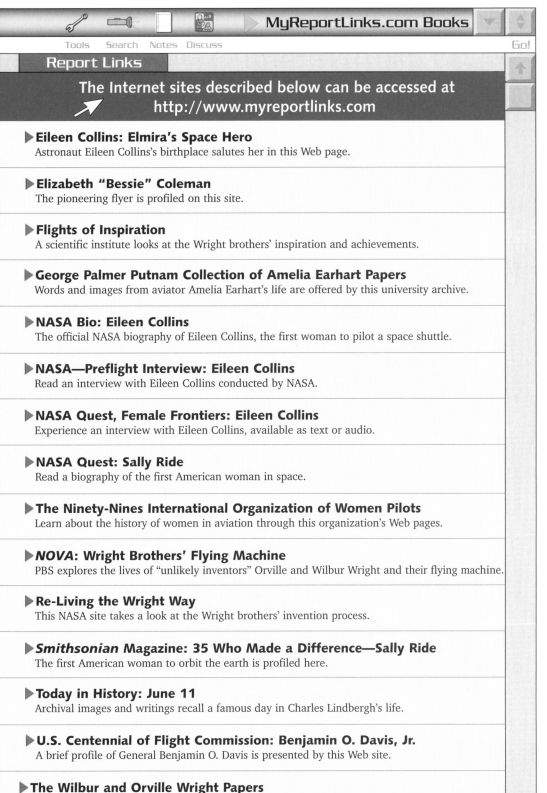

Report Links

The Internet sites described below can be accessed at http://www.myreportlinks.com

▶**Eileen Collins: Elmira's Space Hero**
Astronaut Eileen Collins's birthplace salutes her in this Web page.

▶**Elizabeth "Bessie" Coleman**
The pioneering flyer is profiled on this site.

▶**Flights of Inspiration**
A scientific institute looks at the Wright brothers' inspiration and achievements.

▶**George Palmer Putnam Collection of Amelia Earhart Papers**
Words and images from aviator Amelia Earhart's life are offered by this university archive.

▶**NASA Bio: Eileen Collins**
The official NASA biography of Eileen Collins, the first woman to pilot a space shuttle.

▶**NASA—Preflight Interview: Eileen Collins**
Read an interview with Eileen Collins conducted by NASA.

▶**NASA Quest, Female Frontiers: Eileen Collins**
Experience an interview with Eileen Collins, available as text or audio.

▶**NASA Quest: Sally Ride**
Read a biography of the first American woman in space.

▶**The Ninety-Nines International Organization of Women Pilots**
Learn about the history of women in aviation through this organization's Web pages.

▶*NOVA*: **Wright Brothers' Flying Machine**
PBS explores the lives of "unlikely inventors" Orville and Wilbur Wright and their flying machine.

▶**Re-Living the Wright Way**
This NASA site takes a look at the Wright brothers' invention process.

▶*Smithsonian* **Magazine: 35 Who Made a Difference—Sally Ride**
The first American woman to orbit the earth is profiled here.

▶**Today in History: June 11**
Archival images and writings recall a famous day in Charles Lindbergh's life.

▶**U.S. Centennial of Flight Commission: Benjamin O. Davis, Jr.**
A brief profile of General Benjamin O. Davis is presented by this Web site.

▶**The Wilbur and Orville Wright Papers**
Read the words of the Wright brothers and view archival images from this Library of Congress site.

Glossary

aeronautical engineering—The practice of designing and constructing things that have to do with flight.

aeronautics—Area of study in the field of science that deals with flight.

autogiro—An aircraft that has a propeller for forward motion and a helicopter-like rotor for lift.

barnstormer—A pilot who performs stunts and often races in planes.

command module—The portion of a spacecraft in which the astronauts live, communicate with a ground station, and operate controls during a flight.

conservation—The act of caring for and protecting something to prevent it from destruction, overuse, or neglect.

deploy—To spread out or arrange for a particular purpose.

empower—To enable or permit.

lunar module—The space vehicle that carries the astronauts from the command module to the moon's surface and back.

meteorology—A science that deals with weather and weather forecasting.

mission—An operation designed to carry out the goals of a specific program.

orbit—To make a complete circular path around something.

phenomena—A fact, occurrence, or circumstance that can be observed.

probe—A device that is used to obtain information for exploration.

quasar—An object in outer space that is similar to a star.

segregated—Separated or set apart from others.

simulator—A device used during testing and training periods. It allows the operator to recreate and work with a situation that could likely occur in a real-life performance.

thruster—A jet engine that boosts an aircraft by releasing jet or rocket fuel.

transcontinental flight—Flying across a continent.

transmission—A message that is sent via electro-magnetic waves from one location to another.

wind tunnel—A device used to measure the effect of wind on certain objects such as wings, airfoils, buildings, and cars.

Chapter Notes

Chapter 1. The Wright Brothers

1. Orville Wright, *How We Invented the Airplane* (New York: Dover Publications, 1988), p. 11.

2. First Flight, "Part I—Inventing the Future," *Franklin Institute*, n.d., <http://sln.fi.edu/flights/first/before.html> (March 27, 2007).

3. First Flight, "Flights of Inspiration," *Franklin Institute*, n.d., <http://www.fi.edu/flights/first/intro.html> (March 27, 2007).

Chapter 2. Bessie Coleman

1. Women in History, "Bessie Coleman," *Lakewood Public Library*, n.d., <http://www.lkwdpl.org/wihohio/cole-bes.htm> (March 27, 2007).

2. Vivian Chakarian, "Bessie Coleman Was the First African-American Female Pilot," *Voice of America*, October 22, 2005, <http://www.voanews.com/specialenglish/archive/2005-10/2005-10-22-voa2.cfm?CFID=100681723&CFTOKEN=35485650> (March 27, 2007).

3. Henry M. Holden, "Bessie Coleman," *Women in Aviation*, n.d., <http://www.women-in-aviation.com/ cgi-bin/links/detail.cgi?ID=334> (February 27, 2007).

4. First Flight Shrine, "Bessie Coleman," *First Flight Society Online*, n.d., <http://www.firstflight.org/shrine/bessie_colman.cfm> (March 27, 2007).

5. Henry M. Holden, Women in Aviation Resource Center, "Bessie Coleman," *Black Hawk Publishing*, 1997, <http://www.women-in-aviation.com/cgi-bin/links/detail.cgi?ID=334> (February 27, 2007).

6. "Universal Legacy," *Bessie Coleman*, n.d., <http://www.bessiecoleman.com> (March 27, 2007).

Chapter 3. Charles Lindbergh

1. "Charles A. Lindbergh House—Little Falls, Minnesota," *Charles Lindbergh—An American Aviator*, n.d., <http://www.charleslindbergh.com/house/outside/outside1outsi.asp> (March 27, 2007).

2. Dominick A. Pisono and F. Robert Van Der Linden, *Charles Lindbergh and the Spirit of St. Louis* (Washington D.C.: National Space and Air Museum, Smithsonian, 2002), p. 19.

3. Ibid., p. 20.

4. The American Experience, "Air Mail Maverick," PBS, n.d., <http://www.pbs.org/wgbh/amex/lindbergh/sfeature/airmail.html> (March 28, 2007).

5. Ibid.

6. The American Experience, "The Spirit of St. Louis," *PBS*, n.d., <http://www.pbs.org/wgbh/amex/lindbergh/sfeature/spirit.html> (March 28, 2007).

7. The Flight, "7:52 A.M., May 20, 1927," *Charles Lindbergh—An American Aviator*, n.d., <http://www.charleslindbergh.com/history/paris.asp> (June 4, 2007).

8. The Flight, "Lighting a Bonfire," *Charles Lindbergh—An American Aviator*, n.d., <http://www.charleslindbergh.com/history/paris.asp> (June 4, 2007).

9. Charles Lindbergh Biography, "50 Combat Missions," *Charles Lindbergh—An American Aviator*, n.d., <http://www.charleslindbergh.com/history/index.asp> (June 4, 2007).

Chapter 4. Amelia Earhart

1. Susan Butler, East to the Dawn, *The Life of Amelia Earhart* (Boston, Mass.: Addison-Wesley, 1997), p. 35.

2. Amelia Earhart: A Kansas Portrait, *Kansas State Historical Society*, 2007, <http://www.kshs.org/portraits/earhart_amelia.htm> (July 19, 2007).

3. Butler, p. 40.

4. "Biography," *Amelia Earhart—Celebrating 100 Years of Flight*, n.d., <http://www.ameliaearhart.com/about/biography.html> (June 4, 2007).

5. Butler, p. 85.

6. Ibid.

7. Ibid., p. 394.

8. Ibid., p. 409.

Chapter 5. Benjamin O. Davis, Jr.

1. Benjamin O. Davis, *Benjamin O. Davis, Jr., American: An Autobiography* (Washington D.C.: Smithsonian Press, 1991), p. 28.

2. Ibid., p. 1.

3. Ibid., p. 69.

4. Ibid., p. 94.

5. Ibid., p. 99.

6. Ibid., p. 103.

7. Col. Alan L. Gropman, "Benjamin Davis, American," *The Aviation History Online Museum*, n.d., <http://www.aviation-history.com/airmen/davis.htm> (July 11, 2007).

8. Ibid.

9. Ibid.

Chapter 6. Neil Armstrong

1. The Greatest Adventures of all Time, "To the Moon and Beyond," *Time Magazine*, n.d., <http://www.time.com/time/2003/adventures/amoon.html> (March 28, 2007).

2. Eric M. Jones, ed., from Apollo Lunar Surface Journal, "Apollo 11 Mission Overview," *National Aeronautics and Space Administration*, n.d., <http://www.hq.nasa.gov/alsj/frame.html> (March 28, 2007).

3. James R. Hansen, *First Man: The Life of Neil A. Armstrong* (New York: Simon and Schuster, 2005), p. 46.

4. Ibid.

5. Ibid., p. 48.

6. Ibid.

7. Ibid., p. 93.

8. "A Giant Leap for Mankind," *Time Magazine*, July 25, 1969, <http://www.time.com/time/magazine/article/0,9171,901102,00.html?internalid=AE> (March 28, 2007).

9. Ibid.

10. Eric M. Jones, ed., from Apollo Lunar Surface Journal, "Apollo 11," *National Aeronautics and Space Administration*, n.d., <http://www.hq.nasa.gov/alsj/a11/a11.html> (March 28, 2007).

Chapter 7. Sally Ride

1. John Tylko and Sarah H. Wright, "Sally Ride tells girls about career as astronaut at MIT event," *Massachusetts Institute of Technology*, September 25, 2002, <http://web.mit.edu/newsoffice/2002/sally-0925.html> (March 28, 2007).

2. Science and Exploration, "Sally Ride Interview," *Academy of Achievement*, June 2, 2006, <http://www.achievement.org/autodoc/page/rid0int-1> (February 20, 2007).

3. Ibid.

4. Ibid.

5. Ibid.

6. Ibid.

7. Women of NASA, "Sally Ride," *NASA Quest*, n.d., <http://quest.arc.nasa.gov/people/bios/women/sr.html> (March 28, 2007).

8. Female Frontiers QuestChat Archive, "Sally Ride," March 23, 1999, <http://quest.arc.nasa.gov/people/bios/women/sr.html> (March 28, 2007).

Chapter 8. Eileen Collins

1. Pages in the History of Elmira, "Eileen Collins: Elmira's Space Hero," *City of Elmira*, n.d., <http://www.cityofelmira.net/history/eileen_collins.html> (March 28, 2007).

2. Ibid.

3. NASA Human Space Flight, "Preflight Interview with Eileen Collins," *National Aeronautics and Space Administration*, n.d., <http://spaceflight.nasa.gov/shuttle/archives/sts-93/crew/intcollins.html> (March 28, 2007).

4. Associated Press, "Astronaut Eileen Collins leaves NASA," *MSNBC*, May 1, 2006, <http://www.msnbc.msn.com/id/12578454/> (July 19, 2007).

5. Humans in Space, "STS-114 Commander Eileen Collins: From 'Soaring Capital of America' to the Space Shuttle," *National Aeronautics and Space Administration*, February 11, 2005, <http://www.nasa.gov/vision/space/preparingtravel/eileen_collins_profile.html> (March 28, 2007).

6. Associated Press, "Astronaut Eileen Collins leaves NASA," *MSNBC*, May 1, 2006, <http://www.msnbc.msn.com/id/12578454/> (March 28, 2007).

7. Ibid.

Further Reading

Byers, Anne. *Neil Armstrong: The First Man on the Moon.* New York: Rosen Publishing Group, 2004.

Crompton, Samuel Willard. *The Wright Brothers: First in Flight.* New York: Chelsea House, 2007.

Haugen, Brenda. *Amelia Earhart: Legendary Aviator.* Minneapolis, Mich.: Compass Point Books, 2006.

Holden, Henry M. *Pioneering Astronaut Sally Ride.* Berkeley Heights, N.J.: MyReportLinks.com Books, 2004.

Koopmans, Andy. *Charles Lindbergh.* San Diego, Calif.: Lucent Books, 2003.

Langley, Wanda. *Women of the Wind: Early Women Aviators.* Greensboro, N.C.: Morgan Reynolds Publishing, 2006.

Masters, Anthony. *Heroic Stories.* Boston: Kingfisher Books Ltd., 2005.

Plantz, Connie. *Bessie Coleman: First Black Woman Pilot.* Berkeley Heights, N.J.: Enslow Publishers, 2001.

Raum, Elizabeth. *Eileen Collins.* Chicago, Ill.: Heinemann Library, 2006.

Rinard, Judith E. *Book of Flight: The Smithsonian National Air and Space Museum.* Richmond Hill, Ontario: Firefly Books, 2007.

Index